THE IRISH
COMPANION

Brendan Nolan

A THINK BOOK

Ireland is where strange tales begin and happy endings are possible.
Charles Haughey, Irish Taoiseach

THINK
BOOKS

A Think Book

First published in Great Britain in 2006 by
Think Publishing
The Pall Mall Deposit
124-128 Barlby Road, London W10 6BL
www.thinkpublishing.co.uk

Distributed in the UK and Ireland by Macmillan Distribution Ltd.,
Brunel Road, Houndsmills, Basingstoke RG21 6XS

Distributed in the United States and Canada by
Sterling Publishing Co., Inc.
387 Park Avenue South
New York, NY 10016-8810

Text © Think Publishing 2006
Design and layout © Think Publishing 2006
The moral rights of the author have been asserted

Author: Brendan Nolan
Companion team: Tania Adams, Marian Broderick, Victoria Chow,
James Collins, Rica Dearman, Emma Jones, Lou Millward,
Matt Packer and Marcus Trower.

ISBN-10: 1-84525-028-1
ISBN-13: 978-1-84525-028-7

Printed in Italy by Grafica Veneta S.p.A.
The publishers and authors have made every effort to ensure the accuracy and
currency of the information in *The Irish Companion*. Similarly, every effort
has been made to contact copyright holders. We apologise for any
unintentional errors or omissions. The publisher and authors disclaim any
liability, loss, injury or damage incurred as a consequence, directly or
indirectly, of the use and application of the contents of this book.

Our greatest glory is not in never falling, but in rising every time we fall.
Oliver Goldsmith, Irish playwright

THANKS

Few books are written without the active support and opinion of a slew of people. So, thanks to the following for helping the work along. Any others that are omitted in error and feel affronted by not being mentioned may fill in their own name at the also part and all will be well; we shall rise again.

Thanks to Rita, Rory, Kevin, Alison, Rachel, Josh, and Holly Nolan; Sheelagh Hawkins, Michelle Lunney, Cinta Kenny, Greg Kenny, Jonathan Mullin, Sean O'Neill, Fiona McFadzean, Emma Jones, Ann Fagan, Nuala Deighan, and also...

If Ireland did not exist it could not be invented. It is at once the economic success story of the European Union and a place that recalls centuries-old rural events with an everyday familiarity. It wins Eurovision song contests with ease and in the interval introduces the world to the exotic swirl of Irish dancing and Riverdance.

It is a country that has been invaded on numerous occasions, and generally the invaders stayed on to become more fiercely Irish than those they vanquished. Even its famed Irish fairies are said to be the remnants of one such invader who, when defeated by others, took their magical powers with them into exile underground from where they emerge in force at Hallowe'en.

Its best known export is, of course, Guinness, which began in Ireland in the eighteenth century and is still manufactured at its Dublin brewery for Ireland and the world. It has become the national drink imbibed by local and visitor alike.

Engaging contradictions abound and here begins your exploration with an Irish Companion in hand.

Lovers visit the bones of St Valentine in a Dublin church every February and have their engagement and marriage rings blessed.

Ten Nobel prizes have been awarded to Irish people, four of them in literature. Three went to Irish peacemakers.

The *Titanic* sailed from Ireland on its doomed voyage and Europe was first linked to America by an undersea telegraph cable running out from Co Kerry.

Pilots making the first transatlantic flights in the early twentieth century made landfall in Ireland and an Irishman invented a spidercatcher in the late twentieth century. The Planning Appeals Board has ruled that householders may not store helicopters in garden sheds without planning permission.

These and other stories are to be found in *The Irish Companion*, a book that contains more facts and strange reports than a cattle drover could shake a stick at. Enjoy.

Brendan Nolan, Editor

IRISH WORDS

Craic

The word 'craic' has nothing to do with drugs, although the effect of good 'craic' is much the same as the wellbeing said to be induced by narcotics. 'Craic' is Irish for a good time with lots of fun involved. However, the word can also be used as an interrogative. For example, ask, 'What's the craic?', when you want to know what's happening.

STATUES ON DUBLIN'S O'CONNELL STREET

Daniel O'Connell . . . . *parliamentarian*
Charles Stewart Parnell . . . . *parliamentarian*
Sir John Gray . . . . *O'Connell Street city councillor and MP*
Jim Larkin . . . . *O'Connell Street trade unionist*
Father Theobald Mathew . . . . *temperance priest*
William Smith O'Brien . . . . *revolutionary*
Cúchulainn (inside General Post Office building) . . . . *mythical hero*

NO SMOKE WITHOUT DRINK

Ireland was the first country in the world to have a complete ban on smoking in the workplace. The ban came into effect in March 2004, and it covered all work venues, from hospitals, factories and offices to trains, restaurants and pubs, and even company vehicles.

Hostelries responded to the ban by opening beer gardens for their smoking customers. Some placed half-roofs over the gardens and installed space heaters for the comfort of the addicted. Others, with no space available, asked customers to stand outside the premises to smoke. Wall-mounted fag-disposal units were provided to keep the place butt-free.

However, this practice resulted in the *Garda Síochána* (Ireland's national police force) raiding at least one premises in the town of Athlone where, in the early hours of a morning, after-hours drinking was going on. The illicit tipplers were standing outside on the deserted street smoking, to abide by the smoking ban, before going back into the pub for more drink. A passing patrol car saw them and raided the premises.

A study was conducted two years after the smoking ban was introduced in Ireland by Harvard School of Public Health and Roswell Park Cancer Institute. It looked at levels of air pollution in 128 traditional 'Irish pubs' in 15 countries around the world and found, unsurprisingly, that air pollution from second-hand smoke was 91% lower in pubs located in Ireland, than in those pubs which were in locations where smoke-free laws do not yet apply, such as the UK.

THINK LUCKY

- Ireland's National Lottery was established by statute in 1987. The franchise to operate the lottery was awarded to An Post, the national post office. Net surplus funds are distributed to projects in the areas of sport, youth recreation, health, welfare, culture, national heritage, the Irish language and arts.
- More than €2.4 billion had been given to these projects by 2005.
- In 2005 total sales were €616.4 million.
- The total value of prizes won in Irish Lottery games in 2005 was around €324.8 million.
- In an average week in 2005, some 160,000 Lotto prize-winners were paid; there were 35,000 EuroMillions winners, 300,000 instant game winners and 35,000 TellyBingo winners.
- This gave an average of some 75,000 winners each day.
- Total operating costs in 2005 were 14.3% of sales, or €88.4 million.
- The total operating costs include €38.3 million paid to agents in commission and bonuses.
- Some €203.2 million (33% of total sales) was raised for beneficiary projects in 2005.

THE IRISH CONSTITUTION

The Irish Constitution was enacted on 1 July 1937, and it is called the *Bunreacht na hÉireann* (the Basic Law of Ireland). This is the fundamental legal document which sets out – via a series of 50 Articles – how Ireland should be governed. It also defines the rights of Irish citizens.

In addition to defining all the branches of government, the *Bunreacht na hÉireann* also establishes the courts and sets out how these should be run.

Article 15.4 states that the *Oireachtas* (legislature) must not enact any law deemed repugnant to the Constitution, and that any such law is invalid. If a proposed new law is 'repugnant to the Constitution', it can't be enacted without the Constitution being changed through a constitutional referendum of the citizens.

The Constitution allows for a president and two houses of parliament: the *Dáil Éireann* (166 members called *Teachta Dála* or TDs) elected by universal suffrage every five years, and the upper house of the *Seanad Éireann* (60 members) elected by panels, universities and by nomination (11) of the reigning Taoiseach (the prime minister).

A bookselling chain offered a printing of the Constitution for €2.50 per copy in 2000. As a result, there was a rash of people citing the Constitution to TDs, radio phone-in shows and the newspaper letters pages, until most folk misplaced their copies and calm reigned once more.

CAPTAIN BLIGH IN IRELAND

Captain William Bligh survived being set adrift after a mutiny of his crew, led by Fletcher Christian, on the *Bounty* in 1789.

Safely back in harness, Bligh made his arrival in Dublin in 1800 on a new posting. He was invited to suggest ways in which shipping could make a safe, straight approach up the River Liffey and into the city of Dublin.

A breakwater known as the Bull Wall, extending from the city's Dollymount Strand, was built following his suggestions.

Silting followed the building of this wall, resulting in a sandbank developing into an island – an ideal base for the greens and fairways of the Royal Dublin Golf Club, which shares the island with a long, flat beach enjoyed by both Dublin residents and visitors alike.

Christian and his band of mutineers settled on Pitcairn Island, a long way from Ireland.

Their descendants are still to be found there, and William Bligh's wall still protects Dublin's port.

QUOTE UNQUOTE

Irishness is not primarily a question of birth or blood or language; it is the condition of being involved in the Irish situation, and usually of being mauled by it.
Conor Cruise O'Brien, political writer and academic

IRISH VERSE

I will arise and go now, and go to Innisfree,
And a small cabin build there, of clay and wattles made:
Nine bean-rows will I have there, a hive for the honey-bee,
And live alone in the bee-loud glade.

And I shall have some peace there, for peace comes dropping slow,
Dropping from the veils of the morning to where the cricket sings;
There midnight's all a glimmer, and noon a purple glow,
And evening's full of linnet's wings.

I will arise and go now, for always night and day
I hear lake water lapping with low sounds by the shore;
While I stand on the roadway, or on the pavements grey,
I hear it in the deep heart's core.

William Butler Yeats,
The Lake Isle of Innisfree

Denis Tolam of Cork, who died in 1769, left his sister-in-law four old stockings in his will.

His nephew, Michael Tarles, received two stockings and a nightcap.

Lieutenant Jon Stein received a blue stocking and a red cloak.

Cousin Barbara was left an old boot.

Hannah, sister to the deceased, was left a cracked water jug.

The beneficiaries were somewhat upset with their bequests, having set their hearts on a little bit more. The housekeeper kicked the jug she had been left across the floor. It broke and some coins rolled out.

Soon enough, the others also discovered there was money in their new possessions, and they were happy.

All this goes to show that there is money to be had in old socks, and that we really should be nice to everybody.

A HISTORY OF IRISH EDUCATION

1966 – Maynooth College admits lay students to courses for the first time. Since 1795, the college has been the national seminary for Catholic priests; it has also been a recognised college of the National University of Ireland since 1910. Many people have studied for the priesthood there, but quit once they have gained their degree.

1967 – Minister for Education, Donagh O'Malley TD, introduces free secondary school education. He also gives his approval for a free school-bus transport system.

In the ensuing 10 years, the total number of pupils attending post-primary schools increases from 147,704 to 277,724.

1968 – Third-level education grants are introduced. The grants are based on parental income and a pupil's results in the national Leaving Certificate examinations.

1970 – A long-standing ban on Catholics attending the University of Dublin's Trinity College is lifted by the Catholic Hierarchy.

The ban had been in existence since 1875. Catholic students who wanted to study at Trinity College, which was established under a charter from Queen Elizabeth I, and is located in the very heart of Dublin, had to seek a special dispensation to study there from their bishop – on pain of sin.

1972 – The minimum age to leave school is raised from 14 years of age to 15.

2002 – The minimum age to leave school is raised even higher to 16 years of age.

PENSIONERS' FREE TRAVEL

Free travel on Irish public transport was introduced in 1967 for everyone, irrespective of income, who had reached the pensionable age of 70, an age limit, which has since been reduced to 66 years of age. Minister for Finance, Charles Haughey TD, introduced the measure.

Many used the dispensation to travel to Haughey's funeral in 2006, by which time he had retired from politics, and was in disgrace after a series of revelations that his lavish lifestyle was funded by a number of wealthy businessmen, all of whom stressed they had received no benefit from the former Taoiseach (prime minister) for their largesse.

TALKING MOVIES

When the Alan Parker film of Roddy Doyle's *The Commitments* was released in the USA, a translation was distributed to the American audiences for the 'Dublin-English' language used in it; much to the bemusement of Irish audiences who receive no translation of 'ghetto-rapper-speak' in American films.

MOVING STATUES

Ireland in the middle of a sodden summer of 1984 was quite a depressing place to be, with quite a few graduates going straight from college to the emigration plane for want of employment.

Something had to give.

And give it did. A map that showed 28 locations around Ireland where moving statues had been spotted was published in a Sunday newspaper.

One of the most famous was at Ballinspittle, Co Cork.

A number of locals, who were accompanied by their children, stopped to pray at the statue. While doing so they were alerted by the kids that the statue had, in fact, moved, almost as if it was breathing, or shimmering.

Thereafter, locals turned out in numbers to see for themselves.

Eventually, the size of the crowds grew so big that the local council was forced to widen the road, and coach operators – glad of the work – ferried 'believers' to Ballinspittle for a 'pray and a look at the 'moving statue'.

Television crews, journalists and scientists lined up to discuss the matter. Media from Britain, the US and Australia broadcast and printed the story, successfully putting Ballinspittle on the map.

Even to this day, people travel to Ballinspittle to pray, while others, who are unable to make the trip, send requests to local people to pray at the statue for their intentions.

No miracles have thus far been reported through the intercession of the statues, whether they are either sparkling or still.

BOYS' NAMES

Top 25 babies' names for boys in Ireland 2005

Jack • Sean

Adam • Conor

James • Daniel

Cian • Luke

Aaron • Michael

Dylan • Ryan

Jamie • Ben

David • Thomas

John • Patrick

Matthew • Darragh

Eoin • Oisin

Shane • Alex

Evan

IRISH OBSERVATIONS

Ireland is a country which, during the last thousand years, has maintained a constant struggle against three powerful enemies, and has finally conquered them all.

The first stage of the conflict was that against the Northmen. It lasted three centuries, and ended in the almost complete disappearance of this foe.

The second act of the great drama occupied a period of four hundred years, during which all the resources of the Irish clans were arrayed against Anglo-Norman feudalism, which had finally to succumb; so that Erin remained the only spot in Europe where feudal institutions never prevailed.

The last part of this fearful trilogy was a conflict of three centuries with Protestantism; and the final victory is no longer doubtful.

Can any other modern people offer to the meditation, and, we must say, to the admiration of the Christian reader, a more interesting spectacle? The only European nation which can almost compete with the constancy and never-dying energy of Ireland is the Spanish in its struggle of seven centuries with the Moors.

Augustus J Thebaud,
The Irish Race in the Past and the Present, 1873

Ireland has won the Eurovision Song Contest in 1992, 1993, 1994 and 1996. However, it was the special Irish act in the 1994 contest that gave its performers real long-lasting fame.

Irish duo Paul Harrington and Charlie McGettigan won the 1994 competition by singing 'Rock 'n' Roll Kids' by Brendan Graham; but the real highlight was the Riverdance, which was a seven-minute intermission piece, performed after all of the countries had sung their songs and the votes were being cast.

Produced by Moya Doherty, with principal dancers Michael Flatley and Jean Butler, and Bill Whelan as the composer, the Riverdance was a startling mix of traditional Irish dance, with its rigid body posture and an extravaganza of movement and gesture. The performance wowed an estimated audience of more than 300 million, and a new form of Irish dancing was born.

Subsequently, both Butler and Flatley launched their own musical productions, while the music accompanying the dance was released as a single. It was composed by Whelan for the most part, and featured Irish choral group Anúna, the RTÉ Concert Orchestra and assorted traditional musicians. It went to the top of the charts, and there it remained for 18 weeks, denying victorious Eurovision song 'Rock 'n' Roll Kids' the coveted number one.

A full two-hour show was developed from the original segment by husband and wife team of Moya Doherty and John McColgan; it opened at Dublin's Point Theatre in February 1995.

Three separate touring companies take the show around the world, where audiences have taken it to heart. The three companies employ more than 100 Irish dancers and 60 other performers, along with their crew and support, including medical officers and massage therapists. Dancers have to be at least 16 years of age and at championship level in Irish dancing, preferably having been recalled or placed at world level. The tune 'Cloudsong', featuring Anúna, created an opening motif and was directed by Dublin composer Michael McGlynn. It has featured on all versions since 1996 of the Riverdance album. Anúna left the show in 1996.

The Mayor of San Francisco, Willie Lewis Brown Jr, declared 6 March 2002 'Riverdance Day' in San Francisco on the occasion of the 5,000th performance. The show is still going strong.

QUOTE UNQUOTE

Dublin University contains the cream of Ireland: rich and thick.
Samuel Beckett, Irish playwright

OLD PICTURE, NEW CAPTION

*Jerry often found that winning at cards came down to who
could hold his whiskey better.*

PUBLICAN INFORMATION

Under a 1927 Act of Parliament, some pubs were allowed to stay
open for an hour later than city houses to cater for bona fide
travellers. They were to be located more than five miles from
wherever the drinker lodged the night before. Many drinkers simply
hired a cab and retired there when closing time came in the non-
bona fide houses. The system was abandoned.

NOT SPEEDING

There is a 50/50 chance of not being caught speeding by Irish road
speed cameras.

Half of all photographs from fixed speed cameras are unusable,
according to a report from the Public Accounts Committee.

Faults were still evident in 2005, nearly three years after they
were first identified by the Comptroller and Auditor General, who
found that in 2003, almost half of the 107,000 car images taken
were spoiled.

The rate in 2005 was 49% of the 108,331 images.

The Automobile Association said it was 'shocked', but not
surprised at the findings.

1972

- A constitutional referendum to lower the minimum age of voting from 21 to 18 years of age was carried.

1973

- The Civil Service removes a ban on its female employees getting married.

1976

- Under the Juries Act 1976, all citizens who were aged 18-70, with few exceptions, became eligible for jury service without discrimination based on either gender or property.

1987

- The Status of Children Act, 1987, abolished illegitimacy and granted kids whose parents had not married almost the same rights as those who had.

1993

- Acts of homosexuality were decriminalised thanks to the Criminal Law (Sexual Offences) Act, 1993.

1996

- The Family Law (Divorce) Act, 1996, made divorce available, subject to conditions, following a divorce referendum in 1995.

Between 1996 and 2003, about 14,988 divorce applications were granted in the courts.

2000

- A minimum hourly wage of €5.59 was introduced for an experienced adult employee aged more than 18 years on 1 April. By May 2005, this had risen to €7.65 per hour.

2002

- Life expectancy was around 80.3 years for women and around 75.1 years for men. In 1962 the figure had been 71.9 years for women and about 68.1 years for men.
- The minimum age to leave school was raised to 16 years.

2004

- A smoking ban in enclosed workplaces, including offices, public houses, restaurants, bars, and even company vehicles was instigated.
- The percentage of births outside marriage increased to 32.3% in 2004. This was compared with 14.6% in 1990, 5% in 1980 and 2.7% in 1970. 'Shotgun' marriages and adoptions had both played their parts in distorting the official figures in earlier years.

QUOTE UNQUOTE

The Irish don't know what they want and are prepared to fight to the death to get it.
Sidney Littlewood, British President of the Law Society

18 *Age at which you do not need your parent's consent to join the Irish Defence Forces*

TITANIC MOVIES

As of 2006, the 1997 film *Titanic* had the highest box office take in cinema history. It starred Leonardo DiCaprio and Kate Winslet and featured the theme song, sung by Céline Dion, 'My Heart Will Go On'.

An earlier celluloid telling of the story, which shared the same title, was made in 1953. It starred Clifton Webb and Barbara Stanwyck.

A Night to Remember, made in 1958, also told the story of *Titanic*. This production starred Kenneth More and Honor Blackman.

A GOOD SALARY FOR A POLITICIAN

Politicians' pay per annum (before special allowances and expenses)

Taoiseach (prime minister) – €258,730
Tánaiste (deputy prime minister) – €222,256
Minister – €204,020
TD (MP) – €90,770
Senator – €63,539

WRONG WAY CORRIGAN

Although Douglas Corrigan was born in Galveston, Texas, he was of Irish descent and, inspired by Charles Lindbergh's solo flight across the Atlantic in 1927, resolved to fly to Ireland himself some day.

In 1935 Corrigan applied to the US federal government for permission to make a non-stop flight from New York to Ireland.

His application was denied on the grounds his plane was not deemed sound enough to make a non-stop transatlantic trip.

Imagine the surprise when, on a flight from New York to California, he landed in Ireland, an ocean away, at Baldonnel Aerodrome, in Dublin, following a 28-hour, 13-minute flight.

Corrigan became a legendary aviator, but not because of his accomplishments as a pilot, rather because he allegedly misread his compass.

On 8 July 1938 Corrigan took off from New York on a flight into the clouds when he claimed he read the wrong end of his compass and flew east instead of west.

He was questioned by the authorities and his licence was suspended for the length of time it took him to re-cross the Atlantic by steamship, but he returned to a hero's welcome.

People use the phrase 'Wrong Way Corrigan' to describe anyone who blunders and goes the wrong way, particularly in sporting events, even though, apart from reportedly flying the wrong way, Corrigan was a sound and accomplished pilot.

CABBAGE PATCH PITCHED BATTLE

William Smith O'Brien MP, leader of the revolutionary Young Ireland movement, led a group of peasants in a futile, bloodless battle against police at Ballingarry, Co Tipperary, on 29 July 1848.

The uprising didn't last particularly long and the rebels were defeated. The skirmish became known as the 'Battle for Widow McCormack's Cabbage Patch'.

However, a jury found Smith O'Brien guilty of high treason and he was sentenced to death, commuted to transportation for life to Van Diemen's Land, now known as Tasmania.

IRISH RIDDLE

Which Dubliner became prime minister of the United Kingdom?
Answer on page 153.

IRISH OBSERVATIONS

Or again, after an extremely interesting encounter at the windy hotel with Ireland – that is Mr & Mrs Rowlands; he is a giant, very shapely, small head, obliterated features; she small, abrupt, vivacious. They began directly, & so we talked, – they accepted us as their sort, & were gentry, Irish gentry, very much so, he with a house 500 years old, & no land left. "But I love my King & Country. Whatever they ask me to do I'd do it"– this with great emotion. "Oh yes, we believe in the British Empire; we hate the madman de Valéra." There they live, 14 miles from Cork, hunting, with an old retriever dog, & go to the bazaars miles & miles away. "That's the way we live – no nonsense about us – not like the English people. Now I'll give you my name, & I'll write to my friend & she'll tell you of a house – & and I hope you'll live in Ireland. We want people like ourselves. But wait, till the budget." This she said, with all the airs of the Irish gentry; something very foreign about her, like old Lady Young, & yet in slave to London; of course everyone wants to be English. "We think England's talking of us – not a bit. No," said the obliterated Greek torso, for such he was, "When I was courting my wife – she lived in Liverpool – the young chaps used to say 'Now, Paddy, tell us one of your stories,' but now they don't take any interest in us. But I'd do anything for my King & Country, though you've always treated us very badly."

Virginia Woolf,
The Diary of Virginia Woolf,
Volume IV, 1931-1935

Ireland was one of the quickest of countries in the European Union to adopt the new euro (€), and to consign their old currency (the púnt) to the history books.

Within a week or so of the introduction of the euro in 2002, the Irish populace had embraced this new currency for a majority of their monetary transactions.

On 6 January, the first Sunday following the changeover, church collections were still made up of some 80% Irish currency, but by the following Sunday this was down to less than 20%.

There was a grace period, during which retailers would supply the new currency in change for purchases made with the old money, but most just went to banks and poured the old money onto the counter and exchanged it for the new stuff.

The Central Bank opened on New Year's Day, despite it being a public holiday. At one stage, the line for cash stretched from the front doors of the building for almost 50 metres.

A Central Bank spokesman described it as a 'phenomenal and gratifying response'.

People waiting for new notes were served with Champagne, hot whiskey or tea and coffee as they waited patiently to exchange their punts for the euro.

The bank opened at 10am, but people were gathering from 7.45am. The average wait for cash was about an hour, although the Champagne may have eased the wait for the hardy few.

QUOTE UNQUOTE

When Irish eyes are smiling, watch your step.
Gerald Kersh, British writer

EASTER CUSTOMS

The rising sun dances in the morning over Ireland on Easter Sunday. Children were told not to look directly at the sun. Instead, they gazed at its reflection in water. Adults helped this perception along by surreptitiously nudging the water to shimmer the image.

Eggs were not eaten during Lent. This meant that there was always a surfeit of eggs by Easter for eating, giving away and playing games. Everybody ate (real) eggs on this day. The tradition of eating and giving Easter eggs may date from this time.

Easter Monday was, and still is, a popular day for country marts and fairs. People traditionally relax following the strictures of seven weeks of Lent, which concludes on Easter Sunday.

CAN I STORE MY HELICOPTER
IN MY GARDEN SHED?

The answer to this question is: not without planning permission, according to a 2006 ruling from the Planning Appeals Board.

The ruling stated that the use of helicopters in a back garden, and their storage in a garden shed, constituted material changes of use in planning terms.

Businessman Noel Kearney said his occasional use of the helicopter at his Co Limerick holding was incidental to the enjoyment of his 1.8-hectare home. The machine was occasionally kept in the garden shed, which did have planning permission, he argued. However, neighbouring objectors said helicopter landings were disturbing horses nearby.

The board stated that the planning conditions restricted use of the man's shed to 'purposes ancillary to the use of the house', and which did not include the storage of helicopters.

Kearney said the Irish Aviation Authority had ruled that a 'rotocraft' or a balloon not being used for public transport may take off or land where there was no undue hazard, dependent on the permission of the landowner. In this case, Kearney argued, he was the landowner, but it was all to no avail.

GET BURIED

One of the most expensive places in Ireland to be buried is in Dublin's Mount Jerome Cemetery. It's here that the remains of artist Jack B Yeats and playwright JM Synge lie – although the presence of their bones do not directly affect the cost of a grave.

Plots capable of taking three coffins were priced in 2006 at €7,000. Family plots, defined as suitable for two burials, could be bought for prices in excess of €800.

Those wishing to bury somebody could expect to pay up to €5,000 for a burial plot in other cemeteries. This is because of the high demand for land, allied to a building boom, which forced land prices skywards.

Future corpses thinking ahead had to choose between leaving the purchase of a burial plot to somebody else, or pre-booking a plot and paying more than €3,000 in most places.

Little wonder then that many Irish people are now opting to be cremated, with one in six choosing cremation in Dublin, where facilities are readily available.

For some people, cremation was a financial consideration, while for others, it meant their ashes could be interred in a family plot, which otherwise would not take a coffin. That said, some people just take the ashes home and put them in a glass case near the television!

IRISH WORDS

Quiz

The word 'quiz' is said to have been coined by Richard Daly, a Dublin theatre owner, in the late-eighteenth century as result of a bet that he could introduce a new word overnight. This is said to be a myth by those who choose not to subscribe to this theory.

Daly allegedly persuaded lots of people to paint the four letter word on as many public places as they could in a single night. The result was that many people asked what a 'quiz' might be. Nowadays, lots of pubs have 'pub quizzes', where people drink and answer daft questions in the hope of winning some sort of cash prize.

HIGHEST MOUNTAINS

Highest mountains (by height in metres)
Carrantuohill, Co Kerry, *1041 metres*
Lugnaquilla, Co Wicklow, *924 metres*
Galtymore, Co Tipperary, *919 metres*
Slieve Donard, Co Down, *850 metres*
Mweelrea, Co Mayo, *817 metres*
Mount Leinster, Co Carlow, *793 metres*
Knockmealdown, Co Waterford, *793 metres*
Errigal, Co Donegal, *752 metres*
Kippure, Co Dublin, *752 metres*
Benbaun, Co Galway, *727 metres*

IRISH TRAVELS

Most travellers bypass Islandmagee. The road doesn't lead anywhere except back again, and there is no car ferry to take you over the water to Larne. But it is perfect cycling country; there is little traffic, apart from the occasional Lost Soul, and the hills aren't too steep – although the drops down to Portmuck harbour and the beach at Brown's Bay will burn the rubber on you brakes and change the pressure in your ears. This is a place with a strong sense of community cohesion. 'Kick an Islandmagee man,' the saying goes, 'and the whole limps.' And, beneath the neat and tidy Presbyterian exterior, it is full of the unexpected; there are prehistoric, Gaelic, and Lowland Scottish roots here, twisting together in strange and surprising ways.

David A Wilson, 'Sweet Carnlough Bay'
from *Ireland, a Bicycle and a Tin Whistle*, 1995

*The annual Kilkenny knitting competition was
taken very seriously.*

FLIERS ALCOCK AND BROWN

In our era of instant communication, it's incredibly easy to forget just
how much travelling used to be required to physically get from one
destination to another.

Going from Europe to the United States before air travel arrived
used to involve a sea voyage that would take days.

In 1919, the journey was made shorter by two airmen who carried
some 197 letters entrusted to them by the Newfoundland Postmaster.

Captain John Alcock and Lieutenant Arthur Whitten Brown made
the first non-stop aerial crossing of the Atlantic in a modified Vickers
Vimy IV that year.

They took off from Lester's Field, near St Johns, Newfoundland, on
14 June 1919. They landed on 15 June 1919 at Clifden in the west of
Ireland. The time for the crossing was 16 hours and 27 minutes.

They were presented with the *Daily Mail* prize of £10,000 by
Winston Churchill, who was then Britain's Secretary of State.

The two Englishmen were knighted by King George V in
recognition of their achievement.

NEW BUSINESSES

New businesses set up in Ireland in the first half of 2006 included:
Construction and civil engineering, *1,288*
Real estate, *654*
Property management, *637*
Business and management consultancy, *462*
Software consultancy, *311*

SUPPOSEDLY UNSINKABLE

Although it sank in the last century, before two world wars engulfed the oceans of the world and many lives and ships were lost, the Irish-built ship *Titanic* still exerts a force over many. Books have been written, radio plays broadcast and films made of the fateful voyage of a ship that was so large it was thought to be almost unsinkable.

Titanic was built in Belfast and was designed not only to carry passengers, but also mail between Britain and the United States, hence its full name, *Royal Mail Steamer (RMS) Titanic*. The vessel could accommodate three classes of passenger (first, second and third), and was launched in 1911 at the Harland & Wolf Yard and then fitted out. But *Titanic* never completed a full trip. It sank on its maiden voyage some 400 nautical miles off the coast of Newfoundland, in deep water.

And what a mighty boat it was that sank beneath the waves. *RMS Titanic* measured more than 882 feet long, and was more than 92 feet in breadth. At the waterline the vessel weighed a staggering 52,310 tons.

This weight was carried by a trio of steam engines, with a combined power of 50,000 horse-power, making *Titanic* four times larger than the largest legal classification considered under the British Board of Trade's rules at the time. But *Titanic* was not required to carry more than 16 lifeboats, regardless of the number of passengers and crew onboard, so when it finally sailed, it carried 16 rigid lifeboats and four collapsible boats. This number proved inadequate to the task of evacuating everybody when the vessel started sinking after striking an iceberg on 14 April 1912. More than 1,500 passengers and crew lost their lives when *Titanic* sank.

The Mersey Inquiry, held in Britain after the tragedy, revealed that there were 1,316 passengers on the ship: 325 in first class, 285 in second, and 706 in third. There were 885 crew, making the total onboard the *Titanic* some 2,201. Many people went down with the ship, but others froze to death in the icy sea awaiting rescue. There were some 700 survivors.

POULNABRONE DOLMEN

Poulnabrone Dolmen, Co Clare, is more than 5,000 years old. The three-legged structure is a portal tomb in the middle of a limestone plain. It was excavated in 1986. Among the discoveries unearthed were pottery and jewellery and the remains of up to 22 adults and six children.

FIRST FILMS BY LEADING IRISH ACTORS

Gabriel Byrne, *On a Paving Stone Mounted* (1978)
Pierce Brosnan, *Long Good Friday* (1980)
Colin Farrell, *The Disappearance of Finbar* (1996)
Barry Fitzgerald, *Land of Her Fathers* (1924)
Bronagh Gallagher, *The Commitments* (1991)
Richard Harris, *Alive and Kicking* (1959)
Brenda Fricker, *Sinful Davy* (1969)
Cillian Murphy, *Quando* (1997)
Liam Neeson, *Excalibur* (1981)
Maureen O'Hara, *Kicking the Moon Around* (1938)
Maureen O'Sullivan, *Song o' My Heart* (1930)
Peter O'Toole, *The Savage Innocents* (1959)
Noel Purcell, *Blarney* (1926)

IRISH OBSERVATIONS

On the face of the earth there is no nation in which the love of clean and wholesome sport is more strongly developed than in the Irish. Against us it cannot be urged that we take our pleasures sadly. We enter into them with entire self-abandon, whole-hearted enthusiasm, and genuine exuberance of spirit. There is nothing counterfeit about the Irishman in his play. His one keen desire is to win, be the contest what it may; and towards the achievement of that end he will strain nerve and muscle even to the point of utter exhaustion. And how the onlookers applaud at the spectacle of a desperately contested race, whether between horses, men, motorcars, bicycles, or boats, or of a match between football, hurling, or cricket teams! It matters not which horse, man, car, cycle, boat, or team is successful: the sport is the thing that counts; the strenuousness of the contest is what stimulates and evokes the rapturous applause. At such a moment it is good to be alive. Scenes similar to those hinted at may be witnessed on any sports-field or racetrack in our dear little Emerald Isle almost any day of the year. All is good fellowship; all is in the cause of sport.

Thomas E Healy, 'Ireland At Play'
from *The Glories Of Ireland*, 1914

THE LUCK OF THE IRISH

The shamrock, the unofficial emblem of Ireland, is revered throughout the country for its luck and its simplicity. A three-leaved, young clover, it is said to have derived its importance in Druidic times, when St Patrick came to Ireland to teach the word of God. Asked to explain the doctrine of the Holy Trinity, it is said that St Patrick stooped down and plucked a shamrock to represent a living example of the 'three-in-one'. Today, the shamrock is used as a badge for Irish sports teams, state organisations and many Irish brands.

RECORD BREAKERS

The greatest distance covered by a motorised kart in 24 hours on an outdoor circuit by a four-man team is 1,709.9 kilometres. It was achieved in 1997 at Kirkistown race circuit, Co Down, Northern Ireland.

HOLDING COURT

The Hill of Tara, Co Meath, which is west of Dublin, was the coronation place of Ireland's pre-Christian High Kings. But it was not a hereditary monarchy. Would-be kings either won the crown in battle, or were chosen to take on the role by their peers. Tara was also the location where court was held. No buildings survive there today, but there are quite a few large earthworks left on the hill, some can be found inside an even larger Iron Age enclosure known as a hill fort.

The area has been important since the late Stone Age, when a passage tomb was constructed there. The Hill of Tara was at the height of its power as a political and religious centre in the early centuries after Christ. In 433, St Patrick, who is credited with 'Christianising' the Irish, is said to have defied the pagan priests there by kindling the Easter fire on nearby Slane Hill, while they waited for the official lighting of *Baal Tine* (Baal's Fire) on Tara.

The annual lighting of the fire formed part of a ritual of sun worship. On that night, the fire on every hearth in Ireland was, by law, to be extinguished. Once arrested for his transgression, the media-savvy Patrick went about the task of converting his captors with some degree of success.

Nowadays, Tara is a popular gathering place on 21 June for the summer solstice, where many arrive to celebrate Midsummer's Day and recall pagan times in Ireland. On a clear day from the hilltop, seven surrounding counties can be seen.

The Vikings could lay claim as much as the Celts to being the shapers of modern Ireland.

From about 800, the Vikings were raiding Ireland, Britain and France from their bases in Scandinavia, so come the end of the century, they were over-wintering in Ireland and beginning to colonise it. Dublin began life as a Viking settlement, as did the ports of Waterford and Limerick.

From about 911, the French allowed a group of Vikings to settle in northern France to provide protection against future Viking invaders. These settlers became known as the 'Northmen', from which Normandy is derived. Settled and strong by 1066, these 'Northmen', or Normans, invaded England under William the Conqueror. This led to the Norman Conquest of England.

By 1169, advance armies of Normans from Wales had landed in Ireland, which led to rule from England, a practice that continues to this day in the six north-eastern counties known as Northern Ireland.

It is easy to remember the six counties by the acronym FATDAD: Fermanagh, Antrim, Tyrone, Derry, Armagh, and Down. When Down competes in All-Ireland sports tournaments, their fans confuse opponents by chanting: 'Up Down.'

Contrary to popular opinion, the Normans did not invade Ireland in 1169; they were invited in by local king, Dermot MacMurrough of Leinster to help him in his war against High King Rory O'Connor, who had defeated MacMurrough.

Once in, Norman dominion spread through the centuries, until the entire island owed allegiance to the English crown. All English laws were extended to Ireland in 1210.

The Normans built castles, set up market towns and laid down *their* law. Their feudal system saw peasants granted land by a lord in return for a payment of crops. In turn, the lords were granted land by the king.

Over the centuries, a mixture of Irish and what became known as Anglo-Irish rose in rebellion on a regular basis. The rebellion of 1916, and victories by abstentionist MPs in the British general election of 1918, led to the founding of the Irish Free State in 1922, and of the Irish Republic in 1949. These consisted of 26 counties (out of a total of 32), the other six remaining under British rule.

The Irish Constitution laid claim to the whole of the island and the waters surrounding it. This was dropped in a 1998 referendum when the entire island voted, for the first time since 1922, on a political settlement following the Good Friday Agreement of 1998.

The settlement was agreed and elections were held to a new Northern Assembly to oversee governance of the province.

OLD PICTURE, NEW CAPTION

The luck of the Irish wasn't working for Patrick that night.

QUOTE UNQUOTE

*What's the use of being Irish if the world doesn't
break your heart?*
John F Kennedy, Irish-American, 35th President of the United States

DIMENSIONS

- Ireland is the westernmost island in Europe
- The greatest length (north-south) is 486 kilometres
- The greatest width (east-west) is 275 kilometres
- The total coastline measures 3,169 kilometres
- Carrantuohill, Co Kerry, is the highest mountain
- The longest river is the Shannon
- Ireland's largest lake is Lough Neagh
- Powerscourt Waterfall is the highest in Ireland
- The Ceide Fields, Co Mayo, is the most extensive
  Stone Age monument in the world
- Phoenix Park in Dublin is Europe's largest enclosed park

Blarney

'Blarney' means 'gift of the gab', usually denoting nonsense. Blarney is also a castle in Co Cork where hopefuls lean out on the parapets, over a drop of 120 feet, to kiss a stone. Most folk are unable to stop talking after surviving the experience.

DOGGONE IT

The Control of Dogs Regulations, 1998 impose rules in relation to some breeds and strains/cross-breeds) of dog in Ireland including:

American Pit Bull Terrier • Bandog • Bull Mastiff
Doberman Pinscher • English Bull Terrier
German Shepherd (Alsatian) • Japanese Akita
Japanese Tosa • Rhodesian Ridgeback
Rottweiler • Staffordshire Bull Terrier

The rules state that:

- These dogs (or strains and crosses of them) must be kept on a short, strong lead by a person over 16 years of age who is capable of controlling them.
- They must be muzzled whenever they are in a public place.
- They must wear a collar bearing the name and address of their owner at all times.
- Owners of dogs over four months of age must have a licence.

PHOENIX QUENCHED

The rather suspect practice of closing down one company that owes money and reopening it the next day with nothing changed but the name, while the creditors remain unpaid, was tackled by the new Office of the Director of Corporate Enforcement (ODCE) when it was set up in 2001.

In 2005, one director received a six-month custodial sentence, which was suspended, and eight directors were disqualified for terms ranging from three to five years as a direct consequence of their convictions.

The ODCE requires full accounts of the exact reasons for a company closure, as well as the conduct of any person who was a director of the company during the preceding 12 months.

Improved recording processes of persons who have been disqualified means the Register of Disqualified Persons now contains details of more than 1,000 people.

Until 1979 it was impossible to obtain contraceptives legally in Ireland. It was health minister, Charley Haughey TD, who decided to introduce what he described as 'an Irish solution to an Irish problem'.

The Health (Family Planning) Act, 1979, legalised the sale and importation of contraceptives, which included condoms, on a restricted basis. Under the new law, people needed to get a prescription from a doctor which they could then present to a pharmacist, either of which could refuse to participate on grounds of conscience.

Contraceptives were to be available only for the purpose of family planning, or for medical reasons. And the purchaser was to be named on the prescription.

Any persons found guilty of an offence under this law was liable, on summary conviction, to a fine or imprisonment.

However, family planning clinics dispensed contraceptives in return for donations. The donations enabled them to get around strictures against selling contraceptives before Haughey's solution was made law. In busy towns it was not unusual to see queues forming down a street as people patiently queued for service in these clinics.

The law was amended in 1985 and 1993 to make contraceptives more freely available, and now they can be purchased easily from slot machines and from counter displays.

And you don't have to give your name or even wear a mask.

MODEL ALERT

An alert went up at Dublin Airport in 1998 when a model aircraft landed at the busy location, then parked on a runway taxiway.

A home-designed model aircraft, with a Titan 23cc spark ignition engine, took off from a flying ground in Phoenix Park. According to an official air safety investigation report, the plane's operator on the ground lost command of the aircraft while it was flying circuits.

The model then flew off on its own. When the craft had exhausted its fuel capacity, the miniature plane glided to the ground and landed on the runway at Dublin Airport, without incurring much damage.

A pilot of a Boeing B737, taxiing ready for take-off, spotted the model aircraft nonchalantly parked on a link taxiway, which was near the threshold of Runway 28.

The eagle-eyed aviator reported its presence and airport security personnel swiftly removed it, taking the model craft to the fire station.

The subsequent official enquiry over the incident announced that the probable reason for the loss of command was that the battery in the receiver had been exhausted.

Who operated Ireland's first cinema?
Answer on page 153.

NICKNAMES FOR DUBLIN'S MONUMENTS

Thomas Davis, College Green
Urination once again
Davis composed a stirring ballad, 'A Nation Once Again', and his statue has a fountain feature beneath its feet.

Thomas Moore, College Street
Meeting of the Waters
Moore wrote a song of the same name, and his memorial stands above an underground men's public toilet.

Phil Lynott, Harry Street
The Ace with the Bass
Rocker Lynott died at 37 years of age from drug abuse. He was the front man for Thin Lizzy.

James Joyce, North Earl Street
Prick with the Stick
Joyce famously believed that Dublin could be recreated from his novel, *Ulysses*. His memorial features the writer leaning on a walking stick.

Molly Malone, Grafton Street
Tart with the Cart
The song 'Molly Malone', or 'Cockles and Mussels', is the anthem of Dubliners. Molly was said to be a Dublin fishmonger... or a streetwalker.

Oscar Wilde, Merrion Square
Park Fag on the Crag
One of the most successful playwrights of his time, Wilde was imprisoned after being convicted of gross indecency (homosexual acts).

Wolfe Tone, St Stephen's Green
Tonehenge
Wolfe Tone is the father of Irish Republicanism. His statue was blown up in 1979, although it has since been reconstructed.

**Patrick Kavanagh,
The Grand Canal**
Crank on the Bank
Poet, drinker and writer, barred from many hostelries.

Two Women, Liffey Street
Hags with the Bags
A bronze statue of a bench with two women shoppers chatting. One of the bags was stolen in the early days, but it was returned.

**Fusiliers' Arch,
Stephen's Green**
Traitors' Gate
The arch commemorates the dead of the Dublin Fusiliers, a British regiment made up of Irishmen who fought for Britain.

**Spire of Dublin,
O'Connell Street**
Stiletto in the Ghetto
This dramatic obelisk replaced Nelson's Pillar, which was blown up by the IRA in 1966.

IRISH OBSERVATIONS

There may be many comparisons drawn between English and Irish gentlemen's houses; but perhaps the most striking point of difference between the two is the immense following of the Irish house, such as would make an English housekeeper crazy almost. Three comfortable, well-clothed, good-humoured fellows walked down with me from the car, persisting in carrying one a bag, another a sketching-stool, and so on. Walking about the premises in the morning, sundry others were visible in the court-yard and near the kitchen-door. In the grounds of a gentleman, by name Mr. Marcus C-----rr, began discoursing to me regarding the place, the planting, the fish, the grouse, and the Master; being himself, doubtless, one of the irregulars of the house. As for maids, there were half a score of then scurrying about the house; and I am not ashamed to confess that some of them were exceedingly good-looking. And if I might venture to say a word more, it would be respecting Connemara breakfasts; but this would be an entire and flagrant breach of confidence, and, to be sure, the dinners were just as good.

William Makepeace Thackeray, 'From Galway to Ballinahinch'
from *The Irish Sketchbook*, 1842

QUOTE UNQUOTE

*When I told the people of Northern Ireland that I was
an atheist, a woman in the audience stood up and said,
'Yes, but is it the God of the Catholics or the God of the
Protestants in whom you don't believe?'*
Quentin Crisp, English writer

IRELAND'S FIRST TOLL BRIDGE

The first road toll bridge in modern Ireland opened over the River Liffey in Dublin's docks in 1984. The East Link Bridge can be raised to allow ships to pass up or down the river. An initial reluctance by truckers to pay to cross the river, especially when there were several free bridges within a mile of the bridge, was met by a reduction in tariffs charged for commercial vehicles.

The bridge is the main access route to the Point Theatre, where visiting shows and concerts pitch up. By 2002, total traffic for the year was logged at more than seven million vehicles, with commercial crossings around 982,800. That accounts for about 14% of activity. The bridge also serves as the furthest downstream point of passenger pleasure boat trips on the River Liffey.

A LIGHT ON YOUR BIKE

Failure to use proper lighting on a bicycle is an offence under the Road Traffic (Lighting of Vehicles) Regulations, 1963. Culprits can be hauled before a court of law and duly fined.

During 'lighting-up time', that is, the period beginning half an hour after sunset and ending half an hour before sunrise on the following morning, all cyclists are required to have fitted – and make use of – the following lighting on their bicycles:

- One front lamp
- One rear lamp
- Front lamps (A front lamp means a lamp that is fitted to a non-mechanically propelled vehicle showing to the front a white or yellow light that is visible for a reasonable distance.)
- Rear lamps (A rear lamp is a lamp that is fitted to the rear of the bicycle and when lit, its red light should be visible for 500 feet.)

For those who take their bikes for a walk instead of riding them, lamps do not need to be lit when stopped in traffic, or when a person on foot wheels the bicycle as near as is possible to the left-hand edge of the road.

GIRLS' NAMES

Top 25 babies' names for girls in Ireland in 2005

Emma • Sarah • Katie
Amy • Aoife • Ciara
Sophie • Chloe • Leah
Ella • Emily • Rachel
Niamh • Grace • Rebecca
Hannah • Caoimhe
Ava • Lauren • Jessica
Anna • Kate • Roisin
Lucy • Molly

HANGING

The last public hanging in Ireland took place at Tullamore Gaol in Co Offaly in 1865 when Laurence King was hanged for the murder of Lieutenant Clutterbuck.

Tullamore Gaol was also the scene of the last hanging of a woman in Ireland. Mary Daly was executed there in 1903.

---

34 *Year in the 1800s in which Inglis traveled through Ireland to research one of the most important early social commentaries on Ireland*

Irish teenagers took to wearing T-shirts with a picture of a condom and the slogan 'Just in Casey' when the news broke in 1992 that Eamon Casey, the Bishop of Galway, had fathered a son by his cousin 19 years earlier.

Annie Murphy, 25, arrived in Ireland in 1973 to recover from the break-up of her marriage and to stay with Bishop Casey, 47, in his home. Murphy gave birth to their son, Peter Eamon, and returned with the child to the United States, where she reared him.

The story broke in 1992, and Casey hurriedly left Ireland to begin missionary work in Ecuador. He was subsequently reconciled with his son and with Annie Murphy, and eventually returned to Ireland in 2006 to take up ministry in a rural parish once more.

The seismic change in the attitudes of ordinary Catholics towards the Church can to a large extent be dated from Casey's fall from grace. In the years that followed, scandals involving predatory paedophile priests were revealed that made Casey seem like a caring father in contrast.

Casey was a high-profile cleric and along with another well-known priest, Fr Michael Cleary, he was master of ceremonies in Galway when Pope John Paul II celebrated mass there for thousands of young people.

It was later revealed that Cleary, who died in 1993, had fathered two children with a young woman he took into his house when she sought assistance from abuse.

JIMMY KENNEDY SONGS

Prolific songwriter Jimmy Kennedy was born in Omagh, Co Tyrone.

Some Kennedy songs
'Coronation Waltz'
'The Isle of Capri'
'On the Old Spanish Trail'
'Play to Me, Gypsy'
'Red Sails in the Sunset'
'Rose of Rio'
'Skye Boat Song'
'South of the Border (Down Mexico Way)'
'Teddy Bears' Picnic'
'Waltz of the Gypsies'
'We're Gonna Hang Out the Washing on the Siegfried Line'
'Whispering Serenade'

The Irish can be very protective about their land.

IRISH PROVINCES

There are four provinces in Ireland:

Ulster has nine counties, six of which constitute Northern Ireland

Leinster on the east coast (12 counties)

Munster in the south coast (six counties)

Connacht on the west coast (five counties)

Meath was a fifth province at one time, and the provinces are called *cúige* in Irish from the Irish word *cúig* meaning five.

The Irish living outside Ireland are sometimes said to live in the fifth province.

There are 32 counties in the four provinces:

Ulster: Cavan, Donegal, Monaghan (in the Republic of Ireland), Antrim, Armagh, Derry, Down, Fermanagh, Tyrone (in Northern Ireland).

Leinster: Carlow, Dublin, Kildare, Kilkenny, Laois, Longford, Louth, Meath, Offaly, Westmeath, Wexford, Wicklow.

Munster: Clare, Cork, Kerry, Limerick, Tipperary, Waterford.

Connacht: Galway, Leitrim, Mayo, Roscommon, Sligo.

Arthur Guinness was the founder of the famous Dublin brewery that carries his name. He was born in 1725 in Celbridge, Co Kildare, where his father, Richard Guinness, was a land steward.

Guinness Senior's duties included supervising the brewing of beer for the estate workers. At the age of 34, Arthur acquired a small, disused and ill-equipped brewery at St James's Gate, Dublin, and began his own brewing business. The lease for the site, signed on New Year's Eve 1759, was for 9,000 years at an annual rent of £45.

At first, Arthur brewed ale, but, by the 1770s, he was brewing a new beer called porter.

The brewery is based on the bank of the River Liffey. Canal barges once took Guinness through the canal network to consumers around Ireland or downriver to Dublin Port for loading on ships for shipping around the world.

When Arthur died in 1803, he had amassed a personal fortune of some £23,000 – and he left a flourishing business that later generations of his family developed further.

A job in Guinness was much prized by Dubliners, and generations of families were to work there. Conditions were good and the company was renowned for the benevolent treatment of its workforce, which peaked at 5,000.

The Guinness Archive holds a very large collection of employment records, dated from between 1880 and 1960, which are accessible on request.

The Guinness that is drunk today is made from the same natural ingredients as when it was first brewed. These include:

- Barley
- Water
- Hops
- Yeast

Guinness is currently part of the Diageo international drinks company, and Diageo have developed modern brewing facilities, technical centre services and a logistics headquarters at St James's Gate.

Recent investment in brewing facilities have enabled Dublin to produce close to 12 million kegs of Guinness every year. More than 4,153,846 pints of Guinness are transported each and every day from St James's Gate to customers in Ireland and abroad.

From 2005, all Guinness consumed in Ireland and in Britain was produced at St James's Gate.

Guinness Flavour Extract, the essence of Guinness, is exported from the facility to more than 45 countries across the world, where it is added to a local brewing process to create Guinness for consumption. Using this system, Guinness is brewed in more than 50 countries around the world.

Even as a partitioned small nation, we shall go on and strive to play our part in the world, continuing unswervingly to work for the cause of true freedom and for peace and understanding between all nations.

Eamon de Valera, Irish revolutionary and statesman

SMASHING TRUCKS

Trucks smashed into Irish railway bridges 712 times in the first five years of the new millennium. Irish Rail chiefs said truck drivers were crashing into bridges due to a 'careless lack of attention'.

However, the national rail provider also said that more than 350 out of 415 railway bridges in Ireland had a height clearance of less than five metres – which has been considered the minimum height for tunnels for the last 30 years.

DEER, DEER

- Fallow deer have been present in Phoenix Park, Dublin, since the seventeenth century, when they were hunted for sport.
- The present-day herd is descended from those deer. No new deer have been introduced to the park since 1904.
- The optimum herd population is thought to be some 450 animals. Herd numbers have fluctuated from 1,200 to 38 and back up again.
- Top bucks are tranquillised, weighed and examined before the annual rut and again afterwards for the sake of herd records.
- In all, 15 bucks were dominant in the 2005 rut.

One energetic buck was observed to cover does on 200 occasions on 31 October 2005.
- Best bucks have a harem of willing does to attend to during the rutting season. Contrary to some reports, they do not round up their chosen does.
- In fact, it's the does that choose their favoured buck.
- Male deer may live to be 12 years of age in Phoenix Park, while a female could live to be 20.
- The oldest recorded male died of old age in summer 2004. He was 14. His skeleton was placed on exhibition in the mammal study unit in University College Dublin.

Ireland is a land of mists and mystic shadows; of cloud-wraiths on the purple mountains; of weird silences in the lonely hills, and fitful skies of deepest gloom alternating with gorgeous sunset splendours. All this fantastic caprice of an ever-varying atmosphere stirs the imagination, and makes the Irish people strangely sensitive to spiritual influences. They see visions and dream dreams, and are haunted at all times by an ever-present sense of the supernatural. One can see by the form of the Irish head – a slender oval, prominent at the brows and high in the region of veneration, so different from the globular Teutonic head – that the people are enthusiasts, religious, fanatical; with the instincts of poetry, music, oratory, and superstition far stronger in them than the logical and reasoning faculties. They are made for worshippers, poets, artists, musicians, orators; to move the world by passion, not by logic. Scepticism will never take root in Ireland; infidelity is impossible to the people. To believe fanatically, trust implicitly, hope infinitely, and perhaps to revenge implacably – these are the unchanging and ineradicable characteristics of Irish nature, of Celtic nature, we may say; for it has been the same throughout all history and all ages. And it is these passionate qualities that make the Celt the great motive force of the world, ever striving against limitations towards some vision of ideal splendour; the restless centrifugal force of life, as opposed to the centripetal, which is ever seeking a calm quiescent rest within its appointed sphere.

Lady Jane 'Speranza' Wilde,
Ancient Legends, Mystic Charms,
and Superstitions of Ireland

IRISH RIDDLE

Which Irish writer's creation has appeared in more horror movies than any other?
Answer on page 153.

NATIONAL CAR TEST

Items to be tested in private cars every two years under an EU directive include:

Brakes • Exhaust emissions • Wheels and tyres • Lights
Steering and suspension • Chassis and underbody
Electrical systems • Glass and mirrors • Transmission
Interior • Fuel system • Miscellaneous items

IRELAND AND EUROPE

- Ireland joined the European Economic Community (EEC) at the same time as Denmark and the United Kingdom in 1973, bringing the total membership then to nine member states. By May 2004, the re-named European Union (EU) consisted of some 25 countries.

- Accession Day, 1 May 2004, fell during Ireland's presidency of the EU. Former journalist Pat Cox from Cork was President of the European Parliament on the day.

- With effect from Accession Day, nationals of the 10 new member states of the union were entitled to enter and work in Ireland without restriction. Some other member states controlled access to their labour markets for up to seven years following accession.

- In 2003, almost 50,000 work permits were issued to incoming workers. About a third of them went to people arriving from the 10 accession states of Czech Republic, Estonia, Latvia, Lithuania, Hungary, Poland, Slovenia, Slovakia, Cyprus and Malta.

- Bulgaria and Romania are next to join the EU. Their accession is scheduled for 1 January 2007.

TEN IRISH NOBEL PRIZEWINNERS

William Butler Yeats (Literature) *1923*
George Bernard Shaw (Literature) *1925*
Ernest Thomas Sinton Walton (joint) (Physics) *1951*
Samuel Beckett (Literature) *1969*
Seán MacBride (Peace) *1974*
Mairead Corrigan and Betty Williams (Peace) *1976*
Seamus Heaney (Literature) *1995*
John Hume and David Trimble (Peace) *1998*

A LIBRARY FOR THE NATION

Scot Andrew Carnegie prospered in coal and steel in the United States. In 1901 he sold his business to become one of the world's richest men.

He instigated the Carnegie Free Libraries project whereby communities were grant-aided to establish libraries where there was a clearly demonstrated need. Some 66 such libraries opened in Ireland.

40 ... Foot, the name of previously male-only swimming area at Sandycove, on Dublin Bay. Anybody can swim there now

Dublin is a very considerable city, about one-fourth the size of London, of which it is the image in little – even the streets bear the same names; the beauty of the buildings may dispute for precedence with those of the capital; one is astonished at their magnificence and number. The Parliament House does honour to the nation's representatives; it is an immense circular building surrounded by a magnificent colonnade.

It is worthy of remark that the place where the deputies or representatives of the greatest nation assemble is commonly an old, irregular, ugly building, for which there is such attachment or affection that nobody thinks of displacing it by a new and more commodious structure.

The Bourse or Royal Exchange is somewhat like the Mansion House in London, but smaller. The Customs House is much too fine for its work, and the new building which they call the Four Courts of Justice gives Themis the pleasure to see herself decently lodged, a rare thing in European countries. Her old residence was a frightful place, as much on account of the members as by reason of the lugubrious and sombre appearance of the cave where they practised. I amused myself often by walking among them, and as it was extremely unlikely that I, in my circumstances, should ever have anything to do with them, I could laugh at their big wigs, in which the face is so buried that only a long nose protrudes. They reminded me of hawks dressed to pounce on their prey, with the beaks only visible. If rumour is to be believed, attorneys here yield in nothing to their brethren of our courts; indeed, from certain stories I have heard, it would seem that they are even cleverer.

The squares are large and well built, only the port seems to me to be unworthy of the city. There has just been constructed an immense dock, which will make good certain shortcomings when some houses have been built to protect it from wind. It is singular that the inhabitants have never thought of building a beautiful church here; the churches are all old and without the least decoration. Among them all there are but two miserable bell-towers, and this want prevents the city from having the fine appearance it should exhibit from a distance.

Le Chevalier de la Tocnaye,
A Frenchman's Walk Through Ireland, 1796-7

CHASING THE CROOKS

Widespread revulsion at the shooting dead of the investigative journalist Veronica Guerin on 26 June 1996 saw a renewed police response to a growing problem of organised crime. Guerin was killed on a sunny day in a Dublin suburb. One of two men on a motorcycle shot her at close range as she waited in her car at traffic lights for the light to change.

Staffed by officers from several government departments, the Criminal Assets Bureau (CAB) was established soon thereafter. Its primary objective is to identify and seize assets of those engaged in criminal activity. By the end of 2003, it had seized some €7 million from its targets, many of whom fled abroad to avoid scrutiny.

The Assets Recovery Agency was formed in Northern Ireland under the UK Proceeds of Crime Act 2002. It drew on the experiences of the CAB in its initial stages. It has used its powers to seize the assets of paramilitary and organised crime bosses, often in association with the southern agency on joint investigations.

The border crossing between Northern Ireland and the Republic is the only land border possessed by either Ireland or the UK.

QUOTE UNQUOTE

My Ulster blood is my most priceless heritage.
James Buchanan, Irish-American, 15th President of the United States

DÁIL BAR

Irish parliamentarians were caught with their pants down in 2004 when it was realised that their parliamentary bar had been operating without a licence to serve alcohol. It was estimated that they had been drinking illegally in the Dáil bar for 80 years.

The Government moved to amend the Liquor Licensing Act to provide a licence for the bar and said that it had believed that it did not need a licence because, as legislators, it made the rules.

The Dáil bar has two sections – one for members and another for visitors. Any visitors in search of cheap booze will be disappointed.

In 2006 the Comptroller and Auditor General's office reported that a pint cost only 50 cent less in the visitors' bar than it did elsewhere in Dublin. The audit also raised concerns about the slow rate at which TDs (MPs) paid off their bar tabs and the falling profit margins at the bars in Leinster House.

THE 20 TOP-SELLING HITS OF
ALL TIME IN IRELAND

1. 'Something About the Way You Look Tonight/ Candle in the Wind', Elton John, 1997

2. 'Riverdance', Bill Whelan, 1994

3. 'There's a Whole Lot of Loving Going On', Six, 2002

4. 'Maniac 2000', Mark McCabe, 2000

5. 'Blue (Da Ba Dee)', Eiffel 65, 1999

6. 'Hero', Enrique Iglesias, 2002

7. 'Uptown Girl', Westlife, 2001

8. 'It Wasn't Me', Shaggy, 2001

9. 'Asereje – The Ketchup Song', Las Ketchup, 2002

10. 'Do They Know It's Christmas?', Band Aid 20, 2004

11. 'Perfect Day', Various, 1997

12. 'Angel', Shaggy featuring Rayvon, 2001

13. 'My Heart Will Go On', Céline Dion, 1998

14. 'Stan', Eminem, 2000

15. 'Aon Focal Eile', Richie Kavanagh, 1996

16. 'Can't Fight the Moonlight', LeAnn Rimes, 2000

17. 'Baby One More Time', Britney Spears, 1999

18. 'We've Got the World', Mickey Harte, 2003

19 'Hey Baby', DJ Otzi, 2001

20. 'Believe', Cher, 1998

(Source: www.Irishcharts.ie)

The great Irish Famine, which reached its height in 1847, was, in many of its features, the most striking and most deplorable known to history. The deaths resulting from it, and the emigration which it caused, were so vast, that, at one time, it seemed as if America and the grave were about to absorb the whole population of this country between them. The cause of the calamity was almost as wonderful as the result. It arose from the failure of a root which, by degrees, had become the staple food of the whole working population: a root which, on its first introduction, was received by philanthropists and economists with joy, as a certain protection against that scarcity which sometimes resulted from short harvests. Mr Buckland, a Somersetshire gentleman, sent in 1662 a letter to the Royal Society, recommending the planting of potatoes in all parts of the kingdom, to prevent famine, for which he received the thanks of that learned body; and Evelyn, the well-known author of 'The Sylva,' was requested to mention the proposal at the end of that work.

The potato was first brought into this country about three centuries ago. Tradition and, to some extent, history attribute its introduction to Sir Walter Raleigh. Whether this was actually the case or not, there seems to be no doubt about his having cultivated it on that estate in Munster, which was bestowed upon him by his royal mistress, after the overthrow of the Desmonds.

Some confusion has arisen about the period at which the potato of Virginia, as I shall for the present call the potato, was brought to our shores, from the fact that another root, the batatas, or sweet potato, came into these islands, and was used as a delicacy before the potato of Virginia was known; and, what adds to the confusion, is that the name potato, applied to the Virginian root, is derived from batatas, it not bearing in Virginia any name in the least resembling the word potato. Up to 1640 it was called in England the potato of Virginia, to distinguish it from the sweet potato, which is another evidence that it derived the name potato from batatas. The latter root was extensively cultivated for food in parts of America, but it never got into anything like general cultivation here, perhaps because our climate was too cold for it. It is now only found in our hot-houses, where it produces tubers from one to two pounds in weight.

The Rev John O'Rourke,
The History of the
Great Irish Famine of 1847,
with Notices of Earlier
Irish Famines

MURDER MOST HORRID

Number of recorded murders in Ireland

Year	Number
1950	9
1955	4
1960	3
1965	7
1970	11
1975	23
1980	21
1985	25
1990	17
1995	43
2000	39
2001	52
2002	52
2003	45

IRISH RIDDLE

Which Welshman is commemorated with
a public holiday in Ireland?
Answer on page 153.

TONY DOES FOR SPIDERS

People who do not like spiders yet who do not wish to see them dead may be grateful to a Dublin-born inventor. Tony Allen created his Spidercatcher in the late 1990s to rid his home of spiders without having to splat them. There had been complaints at home that too many were being swiped with a rolled-up newspaper – with the inevitable sorry consequences for the decor.

The Spidercatcher uses two rings of concentric bristles to scoop up a spider. It can be used in even the narrowest corner, and the user is able to incarcerate the spider from arm's length. The arachnid can then be released outside completely unharmed – though whether it will take kindly to forced re-location is another matter entirely.

Allen brought his product to market himself, learning the retail trade as he went along. The Spidercatcher is now available worldwide.

*Year in the 1900s in which Taoiseach Eamon de Valera signed condolences 45
for Hitler's death. Ireland was neutral and Hitler an elected head of state*

When I came back to Dublin, I was court-martialled in my absence and sentenced to death in my absence, so I said they could shoot me in my absence.
Brendan Behan, Irish playwright

IRISH PRESIDENTS

- The office of president was established by the constitution (*Bunreacht na hÉireann*). The president is elected directly by the people.

- The term of office is seven years and a president may not serve more than two terms.

- Former or retiring presidents may become candidates on their own nomination.

- To be a candidate a citizen must be over 35 years of age and must be nominated either by:

  • No fewer than 20 members of the Dáil or the Senate, or
  • No fewer than four administrative counties (including county boroughs).

IRISH PRESIDENTS
Douglas Hyde 1938 to 1945.
Séan T O'Ceallaigh 1945 to 1959.
Eamon de Valera 1959 to 1973.
Erskine Childers 1973 to 1974, when he died in office.
Cearbhall Ó Dálaigh 1974 to 1976 (resigned).
Patrick J Hillery 1976 to 1990.
Mary Robinson 1990 to 1997 (resigned).
Mary McAleese 1997 to present.

ORDERS

The Most Illustrious Order of St Patrick was founded by King George III in 1783 as an honour for the more influential peers in Ireland. St Patrick's Cathedral was the chapel of the order and the Great Hall in Dublin Castle, now St Patrick's Hall, was the chancery where knights were installed and where banquets were held on St Patrick's Day. Each knight had to be a gentleman of blood without reproach and descended of three descents of noblesse. Since independence in 1922, no native hereditary titles have been recognised under Irish law, and no new titles can be created.

THE GREAT HUNGER

The Great Hunger, or the Great Famine, are names given to a catastrophe that occurred between 1845 and 1851. A blight destroyed the potato crop, which provided the staple food for the vast majority of Irish at the time. Many people died of hunger and many others were forced to emigrate in order to survive.

More than a million Irish are estimated to have died in their own country. In addition, some two million emigrated to Great Britain, the United States, Canada and Australia. Many thousands, whose deaths are not recorded as famine deaths, died on the 'coffin ships'.

The potato was grown as a source of food, while other crops were mainly used to pay rent to landlords for a holding. Many of the landlords lived abroad, and their estates were managed by land agents. Failure to pay rent led to the eviction of tenant farmers. During the famine, food was exported from Ireland to meet liabilities to land owners.

Under British penal laws, Irish Catholics had been forbidden to pass the family landholdings on to a single son. Instead, land was subdivided among the male children of a family.

Many males married young and started their own families on their share of land and so contributed to an increased demand for food. Although the penal laws ended in 1829, their effects continued to be felt – with disastrous results.

VICEROY

- The viceroy ruled Ireland on behalf of the reigning monarch. He lived in Dublin Castle, which was the centre of society at the time. When the viceroy moved to Phoenix Park for the summer, a distance of a few miles, society centred on the park. The ruling viceroy was also commander-in-chief of British forces in Ireland.

- Lord Cornwallis served in Ireland as viceroy following his defeat at the hands of the colonists and the loss of the American colonies in the eighteenth century. Cornwallis subdued the 1798 rebellion in Ireland.

- The last viceroy of Ireland was Viscount FitzAlan of Derwent, a Catholic who served in the post until independence in 1922, when the Irish Free State came into being.

The first transatlantic cable was laid between Valentia Island in Ireland and Heart's Content, Newfoundland.

The initial message sent, on 16 August 1858, under the supervision of electrical engineer Wildman Whitehouse read: 'Glory to God in the highest, and on Earth, peace, goodwill to men.'

Shortly thereafter, Queen Victoria sent 98 words of congratulation to US President James Buchanan, which took almost 17 hours to arrive.

By 1853 England was already linked to Ireland by undersea cable, used for morse code. But, the 3,540-kilometre Atlantic stretch posed practical difficulties. The first insulated copper cables were wound with 300,000 miles of iron wire to protect them.

No ship was big enough to carry thousands of miles of cable, so it was loaded onto two ships and spliced in mid-ocean. The laying was finally successful in 1858. However, after only a month of operation, the 2,000-volt system burned through the insulation at a point off the coast of Ireland.

A later attempt saw the *Great Eastern*, the largest ship of its day, carry cable sufficient for a complete crossing along with extra cable to finish laying the cable that had been lost the previous year – if the end could be found by dropping grappling lines into the sea. On 27 July 1866, this cable was pulled ashore at Newfoundland.

The *Great Eastern* then steamed to the point the second cable had reached and found and raised the broken end from a depth of 16,000 feet. On 8 September, the second completed cable was landed, to be followed later by four more cables.

When the system opened for business, the initial rates were $1 a letter, payable in gold, which meant only governments or the very wealthy could afford to use the system. Great brevity in messages was the order of the day long before texting on mobile phones became a twenty-first-century phenomenon. The rate in 1866 for messages became $10 a word, with a 10-word minimum. This was the equivalent of 10 weeks' salary for a skilled workman to send a single message!

The earliest cables could send only one message at a time, but the system increased capacity until it became a feasible, if expensive, communication tool that was open to more people.

OLD PICTURE, NEW CAPTION

Irish fishermen are a famously handsome lot.

AN OLDIE BUT A GOODIE

A series of carvings on a rock at Knowth, Co Meath, has been identified as the most ancient moon map discovered to date. It is estimated to have been carved around 5,000 years ago. Moon trips from Co Meath were not available at that time and so the map was drawn from Earth.

FAMOUS IRISHMEN

George Bernard Shaw wrote his first play at the age of 36, and thereafter wrote 57 plays. In 1935 Shaw was awarded the Nobel Prize for Literature. His last play, Buoyant Billions, was written in 1949, when Shaw was 93. Shaw died in 1950 and in his will left a third of his posthumous earnings to the National Gallery in Dublin.

RELIGIOUS EVENTS

In 1929, thousands of people attended a Pontifical High Mass presided over in Phoenix Park by the Archbishop of Dublin, Most Rev Dr Byrne to mark the centenary of Catholic Emancipation in Ireland. Emancipation was achieved under Daniel O'Connell's leadership in 1829.

Name and number of the Act creating the Republic of Ireland that came into force on 18 April 1949

PUBLICAN INFORMATION

The Vintners' Federation of Ireland represents some 6,000 bar-operating members. In addition, the Licensed Vintners' Association has some 750 members and collectively represents 95% of all publicans in Dublin.

There are a number of other pubs that belong to no grouping but that function just as well.

The number of pub and off-sales licences in Northern Ireland is currently limited to 1,938.

NATIONAL PARKS

There are six National Parks in Ireland:

Killarney National Park, Co *Kerry (10,289 hectares)*
Glenveagh National Park, Co *Donegal (16,958 hectares)*
Connemara National Park, Co *Galway (2,957 hectares)*
Wicklow Mountains National Park, Co *Wicklow (15,925 hectares)*
Burren National Park, Co *Clare (1,673 hectares)*
Ballycroy National Park, Co *Mayo (11,779 hectares)*

TO THE LETTER

Mail delivery in Ireland dates from 1638, when Evan Vaughan, the Deputy Postmaster to Foreign Parts, organised post stages from Dublin to Belfast, Coleraine, Derry, Sligo, Galway and Cork.

The American Pony Express may owe something to Ireland's eighteenth-century practice of transporting mail by post boys who provided their own horses. Until mail coaches were introduced in 1789, posting mail was expensive. There were no home deliveries and mail had to be collected after a conveyance fee was paid at the post office by the addressee. But in 1840 the postal service introduced postage stamps that were bought by the sender, and more people began to send letters.

Between 1855 and 1994 Irish mail was transported by rail on special carriages in which postal staff sorted the mail as the train travelled through the night, stopping at stations across the country. Following a major modernisation project in 1994, the transport of letter post was shifted on to the roads. To assist logistics, the Dublin Mails Centre (DMC), an automated sorting facility, was opened. More than 1.6 million pieces of mail are processed daily by the DMC.

Emigration from Cork to America in the 1840s

Cork is the great outlet of emigrants from the south of Ireland and the Australian Emigration Society have an agent here.

In the month of June, we stood on the quay of Cork to see some emigrants embark in one of the steamers for Falmouth on their way to Australia. The band of exiles amounted to two hundred and an immense crowd had assembled to bid them a long and last adieu. The scene was very touching, and it was impossible to witness it without heart-pain and tears. Mothers clung upon the necks of their athletic sons, young girls clung to elder sisters, fathers – old, white-haired men – fell upon their knees with arms uplifted to heaven, imploring the protecting care of the Almighty on their departing children.

Amid the din, the noise, the turmoil, the people pressing and rolling in vast masses towards the place of embarkation, there were many such sad episodes. Men, old men too, embracing each other and crying like little children. Several passed carefully bearing little relics of their homes: the branch of a favourite hawthorn bush or a bush of meadow-sweet. Many had a long switch of witch-hazel to encircle the ground whereon they were to sleep in the foreign land, so as, according to the universal superstition, to prevent the approach of any venomous reptile or poisonous insect.

On the dock of the steamer there was less confusion than might have been expected. The hour of departure was at hand, the police had torn asunder several who at the last would not be separated, and as many as could find room were leaning over the side of the craft speechless, yet eloquent in gesture, expressing their adieus to their friends and relatives on shore. In the midst of the agitation, a fair-haired boy and girl were sitting tranquilly, yet sadly, watching a very fine white Angora cat that was carefully packed in a basket.

'We are going out to Papa and Mama with nurse', they said in an unmitigated brogue, 'but we are very sorry to leave dear Ireland for all that.' Their father had, we imagine, been a prosperous settler.

It is impossible to describe the final parting. Shrieks and prayers, blessings and lamentations mingled in one great cry from those on the quay and those on shipboard until a band stationed in the forecastle struck up 'St Patrick's Day'.

The communicating plank was withdrawn and the steamer moved majestically forward on her way. Some, overcome with emotion, fell down upon the deck, others waved hats, handkerchiefs and hands to their friends and the band played louder.

**Mr and Mrs Samuel Carter Hall,
'Mr and Mrs Samuel Carter
Hall's Tour of Ireland in 1840'**

*Mary always found her morning dip in the Irish Sea
very invigorating.*

THINGS TO SEE IN OFFALY

The Midlands county of Offaly boasts ideal conditions for migrating birds. It is a regular stop-off for passing flyers during various months of the year. The arrival of migrants from Africa can be observed in April and May all along the southern border of the county. In winter golden plover, flocks of brent, barnacle, white-fronted geese and whooper swans arrive from Greenland, Iceland and Canada.

What TV channel is named after a mythical Irish warrior?
Answer on page 153.

THE LITTLE PEOPLE

The happy leprechaun of tourist delight may have antecedents in a warrior caste. According to the twelfth century *Irish Book of Invasions*, a group of settlers called the Tuatha Dé Danaan arrived in Ireland on May Day, known in Irish as Bealtaine, or the Feast of Bright Fire. They wafted through the air as a host of spirits, says the book, while other sources hold that they came from the west on clouds or through the mists using occult skills and attributes.

The Tuatha Dé Danaan defeated the Firbolgs, the indigenous population, and then the Fomorians. But they fell in a third great battle against invading Milesians, early Celts from Spain who smeared their naked bodies with bright war paint and fought ferociously. Defeated, the Dé Danaan went underground into the fairy mounds, or *sidhe*, where some say they remain as *sluagh sidhe*, the Fairy Host.

Known as 'the little people', some believe they occasionally intervene in human trouble on the side of justice and righteousness, armed with invisibility, flaming lances and magical shields; others tell tales of meeting the Phouca, or Pooka, a bad being who can take the shape of a human or an animal as it chooses.

Many stories tell of them taking a human child and leaving in its place a changeling – an infant that usually has a physical or mental defect. William Butler Yeats wrote such a story in 'To the Waters and the Wild', a poem that relates the abduction of a human child, hand in hand with a fairy, to the waters and the wild.

According to legend, the little people live in or near hawthorn trees. As a result, the hawthorn, especially the lone bush, has always been regarded with a mixture of fear and respect by country people. Tales abound of fairy trees causing misfortune to those who damage or destroy them. Modern road building and development projects have often taken into account the location of a hawthorn tree.

The native hawthorn tree is called the May bush because of its time of flowering. In the 1999-2001 survey, the Tree Register of Ireland recorded a hawthorn tree near Bennekerry in Co Carlow that is estimated to be about 300 years old. It is a single-stemmed tree with a trunk girth of 2.4 metres.

THE NATIONAL ANTHEM

Ireland's national anthem is 'The Soldier's Song' – or, in Irish, 'Amhran na bhFiann'. It is sung in Irish – the English translation only being for those who do not understand the language.

The anthem was written in 1907 by Peadar Kearney, an uncle of the writer Brendan Behan. It was first published in the newspaper *Irish Freedom* in 1912, but was not widely known until sung at the General Post Office during the Easter Rising of 1916. Its militant lyrics declare readiness to fight on behalf of Ireland.

The chorus was formally adopted as the national anthem in 1926.

A section of the national anthem, consisting of the first four bars followed by the last five, is also the 'Presidential Salute'.

The salute is played when the president arrives somewhere, usually at a public occasion, like a sports event. It usually means the match will start soon and so engenders excitement among assembled citizens when heard.

QUOTE UNQUOTE

The Irish are not in a conspiracy to cheat the world by false representations of the merits of their countrymen. No, sir, the Irish are a fair people – they never speak well of one another.
Dr Samuel Johnson, English poet, critic and writer

THE OFFICIAL EMBLEM

The harp is the universal emblem of the state at home and abroad. It is always used by government departments and offices. It also appears on all Irish coins. No head of state appears on Irish coins.

The harp is engraved on the seal of office of the president and it is also on the president's flag, where it appears as a gold harp with silver strings on blue. The harp faces right in official manifestations.

The design of the harp is based on a harp known as 'Brian Boru's harp', after an eleventh-century king. This fifteenth-century instrument is preserved in the museum of Trinity College, Dublin.

Guinness, a brewer of beer, uses the same harp as a company logo to identify its products, but its harp faces left, as any imbiber well knows.

RECORD BREAKERS

The youngest footballer to play in a World Cup match is Norman Whiteside, who was 17 years and 41 days old when he played for Northern Ireland against Yugoslavia. The match was played on 17 June 1982. Whiteside also played for Manchester United, and later for Everton.

YOU LUCKY *SAOI*

Saoi is the highest honour that members of Aosdána, the affiliation of artists in Ireland, can bestow upon a fellow member. No more than five living members can be so honoured at one time. The title of *Saoi* is conferred by the President of Ireland.

Current Saoi *(2006)*
Benedict Kiely • Louis le Brocquy
Seamus Heaney • Anthony Cronin
Brian Friel

Former Saoi
Samuel Beckett • Mary Lavin
Seán Ó Faoláin • Francis Stewart
Patrick Collins • Tony O'Malley

MADE IN IRELAND... ALMOST

John Boyd Dunlop was a veterinary surgeon by profession, having qualified at Edinburgh University when he was only 19, but he will be better remembered for his invention of the pneumatic tyre, which he first used to win a bicycle race at Queen's College Sports in Belfast in 1889.

In 1887 Dunlop had patented a design based on an inflated rubber tube. However another Scot, Robert William Thomson, patented a pneumatic design in 1845 and the two engaged in legal battles over their inventions. Despite Thomson's earlier work,

it is Dunlop who is credited with the invention of the modern rubber tyre.

As with many inventors, Dunlop did not benefit much materially from his invention. He set up what would become the Dunlop Rubber Company, but sold the patent and company name early on.

A Dunlop factory was established in Dublin in 1889, and a larger factory operated in Cork City until its business moved to Birmingham in the 1980s. Dunlop died in Dublin in 1921.

The age at which you qualify for Golden Years discounts in 55 Ireland's hotels

KILLORGLIN PUCK FAIR

An annual fair in the heart of Co Kerry can generate as much as €6 million for the local community as some 100,000 people pass through Killorglin during the three days of Puck Fair.

The August fair is one of Ireland's oldest and longest celebrated local festivals. Events include the traditional horse fair, open-air night concerts, a fireworks display, children's competitions, street entertainers, dancing displays, and parade and coronation ceremony of King Puck, a wild goat captured for the purpose.

It has been suggested that the fair originates from pre-Christian celebrations of a fruitful harvest and that the male goat, or 'Puck', was a pagan symbol of fertility, like the pagan god Pan. However, there are many other theories too, and accurate knowledge about the precise origins of the fair has been lost over the years.

None of which bothers overmuch the assembled masses as they party their way through August.

DUBLIN TRAMS

Electric trams were introduced to Dublin in 1896, and by 1902 horse-drawn trams were a thing of the past.

Dublin's first electric trams ran between Haddington Road and Dalkey, and their operation was taken over by the Dublin United Tramways, at that time running about 170 horse cars over 33 route miles. The last horse tram ran on the Bath Avenue line in January 1901.

On some electrified routes, express trams had a length over which they ran for nearly four and a half miles non-stop. Double-deck trams used on the streets of Dublin were built at Spa Road Works in Inchicore. Demand for the service declined, however, and the last route to run was the Howth summit tram which gave up the ghost in 1959.

In the years that followed, tram lines were removed from the city streets and supporting poles for overhead lines were cannibalised in places for street light standards.

Single-deck trams came back in 2004 when Luas, a light rail transit (LRT) system, connected suburban parts of Dublin with the city centre on two separate tramlines.

However, the Red and Green lines do not connect. There is a 15-minute walk for passengers between St Stephen's Green on the Green Line and Abbey Street on the Red Line.

SAILING AHEAD

Co Clare-born John Philip Holland won an 1888 US Government design competition for a military submarine – however, he fell out with naval designers and his design was abandoned. Born in 1841, Holland began designing submarines after emigrating to New Jersey. His first sub sank after someone forgot to install screw plugs. He went on to design subs 'suitable for war'. He invented a mechanism for submariners to evacuate their sinking vessel, showing both a faith and lack of it in his designs.

QUOTE UNQUOTE

The Irish gave the bagpipes to the Scots as a joke,
but the Scots haven't seen the joke yet.
Oliver Herford, American writer

IRISH OBSERVATIONS

No record of the glories of Ireland would be complete without an effort, however inadequate, to analyze and illustrate her wit and humour. Often misunderstood, misrepresented, and misinterpreted, they are nevertheless universally admitted to be racial traits, and for an excellent reason. Other nations exhibit these qualities in their literature, and Ireland herself is rich in writers who have furnished food for mirth. But her special pre-eminence resides in the possession of what, to adapt a famous phrase, may be called an *anima naturaliter jocosa*. Irish wit and Irish humour are a national inheritance. They are inherent in the race as a whole, independent of education or culture or comfort. The best Irish sayings are the sayings of the people; the greatest Irish humorists are the nameless multitude who have never written books or found a place in national dictionaries of biography. None but an Irishman could have coined that supreme expression of contempt: 'I wouldn't be seen dead with him at a pig-fair,' or rebuked a young barrister because he did not 'squandher his carcass' (ie, gesticulate) enough. But we cannot trace the paternity of these sayings any more than we can that of the lightning retort of the man to whom one of the 'quality' had given a glass of whisky. 'That's made another man of you, Patsy,' remarked the donor. 'Deed an' it has, sor,' Patsy flashed back, 'an' that other man would be glad of another glass.' It is enough for our purpose to note that such sayings are typically Irish and that their peculiar felicity consists in their combining both wit and humour.

Charles L Graves,
'Irish Wit and Humour'
from *The Glories of Ireland*

THE NATIONAL FLAG

The national flag of Ireland is a tricolour of green, white and orange. The flag is twice as wide as it is high. The three colours are of equal size and the green goes next to the flagstaff. The flag was first introduced in 1848 by Thomas Francis Meagher, who based it on the French tricolour.

Green represents the older tradition while orange represents the supporters of William of Orange. The white in the centre signifies a lasting peace between the orange and green.

The tricolour came to be regarded as the national flag when it was raised above the General Post Office in Dublin during the Easter Rising of 1916. It is now enshrined in the constitution of Ireland.

Northern Ireland uses the union flag, the Union Jack, as its official flag. The flag of the province of Ulster, which is based on the crest of the O'Neill chieftains of Ulster, is favoured by some Northerners at sporting occasions.

PUBLIC ARTWORK

Irish county councils provide funding for public art under a scheme whereby a percentage of the cost of public infrastructural funding is allocated to art.

Some of this public art is in Dublin:
Cinema Usher – Hawkins Street
Strong Striking Bear – Irish Financial Services Centre
A Cow – Jervis Street
Two Children – Portland Row
A Hand – Marlborough Street
Two Deer – N11 Glen of the Downs

LOVE ME DEARLY

Charles Stewart Parnell was the charismatic leader of the Irish Home Rule movement in the late nineteenth century when he fell in love with a married woman. Kitty O'Shea was the wife of Captain O'Shea, who filed for divorce in 1889, citing the unmarried Parnell as co-respondent. The ensuing furore led to a split in Parnell's party and he died two years later.

DEPARTED STATUES

A statue of Lord Hugh Gough was the target of a sustained IRA campaign in the 1950s. It was eventually removed from the main road of Phoenix Park when it was damaged by yet another explosion in 1957. Winston Churchill remembered his grandfather, John Winston Spencer Churchill, Duke of Marlborough, addressing the gathered crowd as he unveiled the equestrian statue in 1878. Today, a Christmas tree occupies its former spot each Christmas.

IRISH RIDDLE

Who was the first Irish-born writer to win the
prestigious Booker prize for fiction?
Answer on page 153.

Answer on page 153.

GUBU

It is not often that a murder gives rise to a new acronym, but then it is not often that a murderer is caught staying in the apartment of the serving attorney general by investigating police.

Man about town Malcolm MacArthur was caught and convicted of the murder of nurse Bridie Gargan. She was bludgeoned to death by MacArthur as he attempted to steal her car on 22 July 1982.

MacArthur was arrested on 17 August at the Co Dublin home of the then attorney general, Patrick Connolly. The arrest at his home led to major political repercussions. The unsuspecting Connolly was ordered back from holiday by the serving Taoiseach, Charlie Haughey, when the story broke.

Asked to comment on the arrest, Haughey said the attorney general was the person that he would ordinarily ask for advice in such a situation. He declared the case to be 'grotesque, unbelievable, bizarre and unprecedented', giving rise to the acronym GUBU to describe such an occurrence.

In a further twist, the serving Minister for Justice, Michael McDowell TD, passed the case onto his Junior Minister, Willie O'Dea TD, to review when MacArthur's petition for parole came before him in 2005.

McDowell had been a junior member of MacArthur's defence team at his trial – at which the defendant pleaded guilty. MacArthur is still in prison today, which means that he is one of Ireland's longest-serving inmates.

Phoenix Park has been a part of Dublin and Ireland since the seventeenth century. A vast enclosure of 709 hectares, it contains many recreational facilities, including Furry Glen, a protected area situated in the designated wilderness area. The park is also a bird sanctuary.

The park used to be known for its red squirrels, but the last recorded sighting of one was on St Patrick's Day in 1987. By the turn of the millennium, no red squirrels lived there any more. However, Dublin Zoo, which is also located within the park, is planning to breed and re-introduce some 300 reds.

The first recorded sighting of the more aggressive American grey squirrel was in 1978. It was introduced to Ireland in 1911 as a wedding present and released in Longford. The grey has no natural predators and can consume squirrel food at an earlier stage than can the red. As a consequence, the red died off across much of the country.

Under British rule, Phoenix Park was the home of the three most powerful men in Ireland: the lord lieutenant, the chief secretary, and the under secretary. Today it is the home of the president of Ireland and the ambassador of the United States.

Until a few years ago, Phoenix Park's visitor centre was the residence of the papal nuncio, the representative of the Vatican in Ireland.

The park houses the headquarters of the Garda Síochána, the national police force, and is the headquarters of the national defence forces.

No two buildings in Phoenix Park have the same design. Some, like the lodges in Áras an Uachtaráin, the home of the president, carry old names, such as the Henman's Lodge or the Cowman's Lodge, to recall former use.

There is a major public hospital in the park at St Mary's. It sheltered the orphaned and abandoned children of British soldiers and in later times played its part in the war against TB. It now caters for a population of elderly patients.

Once a suburb of Dublin city and a place to visit in order to escape from the smoky city, Phoenix Park currently faces pressures that were undreamt of in the seventeenth century, when it was first conceived of as a royal deer park.

Most of the pressure comes from commuters. By the year 2000, some 30,000 cars were using the park as an access route every day, causing major pollution and no little frustration to the park's other users.

OLD PICTURE, NEW CAPTION

The whole bar turned to stare whenever a stranger walked in.

FLYING BOATS IN THE ESTUARY

It may be hard to believe today, but great big aeroplanes used to fly from the United States to Ireland and land in Shannon harbour. The brief era of the flying boats, which began in the late 1930s and ended in the 1940s, is catalogued in a €2 million museum in the Shannon port of Foynes, Co Limerick.

The centrepiece of the museum is a full-size replica of a Boeing 314 flying boat, which was nicknamed the 'Yankee Clipper'. With a maximum speed of 210mph, Yankee Clippers were the fastest civil aircraft to cross the Atlantic during World War II. Only 12 Yankee Clippers were ever built.

In its heyday, Foynes was visited by world leaders and film stars, who were the glamorous passengers on Yankee Clippers that splash-landed there for refuelling stops, as they flitted between Europe and the United States.

The Yankee Clipper was regarded as the Concorde of its day – and it even had a honeymoon suite!

WEATHER OBSERVATION STATIONS

1 Belmullet
2 Birr
3 Claremorris
4 Clones
5 Kilkenny
6 Malin Head
7 Mullingar
8 Rosslare

QUOTE UNQUOTE

Ireland is a fruitful mother of genius, but a barren nurse.
John Boyle O'Reilly, Irish poet and novelist

IRISH TRAVELS

'How Shannon Acquired its Name'

A long time ago there was a well in Ossory, shaded by a rowan tree. When the berries became ripe they would drop Into the water, and be eaten by the salmon that had their residence in the well. Red spots would then appear on the fish, and they received the name of 'Salmon of Knowledge.' It was not so easy to take these salmon, for there were shelving banks, and they could also retreat into the cavern from which issued the waters that supplied the well. However, one was occasionally caught, and the captor, so soon as he had made his repast on it, found himself gifted with extraordinary knowledge, even as Fion, son of Cumhail, when he had tasted of the broiled salmon of the Boyne. It was understood that no woman could taste of this delicacy and live. Yet Sionan, a lady cursed with an extraordinary desire of knowledge, braved the danger, suspecting the report to be spread abroad and maintained by the male sex from merely selfish motives. So, in order to lose no time, she had a fire ready by the side of the well, and the unfortunate fish was scarcely flung out on the herbage when he was disembowelled and frying on the coals. Who can describe the rapture she felt from the burst of light that filled her mind on swallowing the first morsel. Alas, the next moment she was enveloped by the furious waters, which, bursting forth, swept westwards, and carried the unfortunate lady with them, till they were lost in the great river which ever after bore her name.

Patrick Kennedy, *Legendary Fictions of the Irish Celts,* 1891

IRISH COFFEE

Irish coffee was concocted at Foynes harbour, Co Limerick, during World War II. It was first served as welcome drink to travellers coming ashore from the flying boats travelling between Europe and the United States. Not surprisingly, there is now an annual Irish coffee festival in Foynes.

IRISH COFFEE
Ingredients
1 measure of Irish whiskey
1 teaspoon of raw sugar
1 heaped dessert spoon of whipped cream
Hot, strong coffee to fill the glass to about one inch of the rim

Concocting
1. Pre-warm a stemmed whiskey glass.
2. Add the whiskey.
3. Add the sugar and stir in the coffee.
4. Pour the whipped cream down the neck of the bowl of a teaspoon, so it floats on the coffee. Do not stir after adding the cream.
5. Say *Sláinte*.
6. Drink the coffee through the cream.

BANNED IN IRELAND

Lee Dunne claims to be the most banned writer in Ireland. Seven of his sexy, humorous books and two of his films, *Paddy* and *Wedding Night*, have been banned in his native country. The first of his books to be banned was *Paddy Maguire is Dead* (1972), and he was subsequently unable to get a book published in Ireland until the late 1980s.

Paddy Maguire is Dead was eventually published in Ireland in 2006 – some 34 years after the initial ban. Dunne was 72 years old by then and still writing. He said the novel was not primarily a 'horny' book, but dealt with alcoholism and a man's battle with promiscuity and drink.

Also banned were *Midnight Cabbie*, *The Day of the Cabbie*, *The Cabbie Who Came in From the Cold*, *The Virgin Cabbies*, and Dunne's own favourite, *The Cabfather*. The Irish film censor banned *Paddy*, the Hollywood movie of *Goodbye to the Hill* (1965), a Dunne book that was not banned.

Undeterred, Dunne adapted *Goodbye to the Hill* for the stage where it was a commercial success. There was, and is, no censorship of theatre in Ireland.

ORDERS

The Order of the Knights of St Columbanus was founded in Belfast in 1915 by Father James K Cannon O'Neill. Ely House in Central Dublin has served as its headquarters since 1923.

Membership is open to Catholic males aged 21 or over. While the order is not a secret organisation, its membership and affairs are confidential to the members, who must be practising Catholics as defined by the church. Prospective new members are nominated by an existing member to join a particular primary council.

IRISH TRAVELS

He told the doctor he was due in the barroom at eight o'clock in the morning; the barroom was in a slum in the Bowery; and he had only been able to keep himself in health by getting up at five o'clock and going for long walks in the Central Park.

'A sea voyage is what you want,' said the doctor. 'Why not go to Ireland for two or three months? You will come back a new man.'

'I'd like to see Ireland again.'

And he began to wonder how the people at home were getting on. The doctor was right. He thanked him, then three weeks after he landed in Cork.

As he sat in the railway carriage he recalled his native village, built among the rocks of the large headland stretching out into the winding lake. He could see the houses and the streets, and the fields of the tenants, and the Georgian mansion and the owners of it; he and they had been boys together before he went to America. He remembered the villagers going every morning to the big house to work in the stables, in the garden, in the fields – mowing, reaping, digging, and Michael Malia building a wall; it was all as if it were yesterday, yet he had been thirteen years in America; and when the train stopped at the station the first thing he did was to look round for any changes that might have come into it.

It was the same blue limestone station as it was thirteen years ago, with the same five long miles between it and Duncannon. He had once walked these miles gaily, in little over an hour, carrying a heavy bundle on a stick, but he did not feel strong enough for the walk today, though the evening tempted him to try it.

George Moore, 'Home Sickness'
from _The Untilled Field_

BLOOMSDAY

On 16 June every year, Dubliners and others around the world celebrate something that never really happened.

Known as 'Bloomsday', 16 June is an occasion for people to dress up in period costume and recreate scenes from the novel *Ulysses* by James Joyce.

All the action in the book is set in Dublin on that date. It is the day when, in 1904, Joyce first walked out with Nora Barnacle, who was destined to become his wife.

Joyce began work on *Ulysses* in 1914 after the publication of *A Portrait of the Artist as a Young Man*, and it was eventually published in 1922. It consists of 18 chapters.

The narrative parallels Homer's *The Odyssey* – as does the Coen Brothers' film, *O Brother Where Art Thou?* (2000). However, an in-depth knowledge of *The Odyssey* is not necessary for enjoyment of either the book or the film.

The main character in *Ulysses* is Leopold Bloom in whose honour Bloomsday is named. A non-practising Jew, he represents the hero Ulysses.

Molly Bloom, Leopold's wife, is equated with Penelope in *The Odyssey*, and the last chapter of the book is dedicated solely to her musings.

Molly's famous soliloquy, which concludes the book, is original and striking in its portrayal of a voluptuous, sensual woman. It poses a sizeable challenge to any actress contemplating including it in a one-woman show.

It runs to a total of 62 pages of the Bodley Head edition and lacks any punctuation.

QUOTE UNQUOTE

St Patrick... one of the few saints whose feast day presents the opportunity to get determinedly whacked and make a fool of oneself all under the guise of acting Irish.
Charles Madigan, American newspaperman

IRISH SOCCER

Under manager Jack Charlton the Irish soccer team qualified for the 1988 European Championships – their first ever major finals. Ireland won an opening game against England then drew with the Soviet Union. However, in the final group match against Holland, Ireland was defeated. More than 200,000 people lined the streets of Dublin to welcome the team home.

BROWN GOLD

Ireland has few coal reserves and what little there is does not suit a domestic fire very well. However, there are large areas of bogland around the country, and turf from these has been used as fuel for centuries. Today, mechanised turf production is big business.

In the Bog of Allen in the Midlands, the tradition of turf cutting by hand goes back 400 years – and continues today on smaller holdings. A tool called a *sleán* is used to cut sods of turf, which are then stacked to dry in a process called 'footing'.

On the industrial side, a moss peat factory opened and peat briquette factories were set up in Co Kildare. During World War II, when coal imports ceased, the Irish army camped in the Bog of Allen and manually cut the turf. The dried sods were brought to Dublin by barge on the Grand Canal and stacked in Phoenix Park for distribution as part of wartime rations.

Bord na Móna, or the Irish Turf Board, is a state-owned company set up in 1946 to commercially develop peat resources. It has used up some 85,000 hectares of peatland for a domestic fuel mainly in the form of compressed briquettes, electricity generation and horticultural products.

HOLY DAYS IN IRELAND

(Not public holidays but observed as such, particularly in rural areas.)

Immaculate Conception (8 December)
Epiphany (6 January)
St Patrick (17 March)
Assumption of Our Lady (15 August)
All Saints (1 November)

EUROVISION

Johnny Logan had the first of three Eurovision successes in 1980 when he performed 'What's Another Year', written by Shay Healy, at the contest held in The Hague, Netherlands, and was voted number one by the judges. His second success followed in 1987 – this time in Brussels. Logan won the competition with 'Hold Me Now', which he had written himself. His third Eurovision triumph came in 1992 in Malmo, Sweden, when Linda Martin won the contest with 'Why Me?', another song penned by Logan.

Age at which retirees receive a pension and a free travel pass

RYANAIR PHOTO-ID FLIGHTS

To fly Ryanair you need one of the following:

- A valid passport.

- A valid government-issued national identity card from a European Economic Area (EEA) country.

- A national identity card issued by the government of Gibraltar.

- A valid UN Refugee Convention Travel Document, issued by a government in place of a valid passport, is acceptable.

- A valid EEA driving licence with photo, presented by a passenger whose place of birth is within the EEA, is acceptable only for travel on internal flights within the UK, internal flights within Italy, and flights between the UK and Republic of Ireland.

MY KINGDOM FOR A BULL

The Táin is an exciting saga that tells the story of the Cattle Raid of Cooley in an Ireland of about 500BC. It deals with the conflict between the provinces of Connacht and Ulster for possession of a prize bull.

Ireland was divided into five provinces at the time. Today there are four.

Maeve, the queen of Connacht, quarrelled with her husband, Ailill, over who had the most wealth. Ailill did not like the suggestion that he was a kept man, and he was able to successfully argue that he was, in fact, better off than his wife by pointing out that he owned a superb white bull.

Maeve was envious and decided that ownership of the famed Brown Bull of Cooley would give her the upper hand. She went to war to take it.

Standing in her way was the fearsome warrior Dearg Doom, also known as Cúchulainn. As the only Ulsterman who was immune from a curse that had afflicted his kinsmen with a sickness, Cúchulainn took on the defence of Ulster on his own. He agreed to fight all-comers in single combat – provided Maeve's army did not advance while he fought.

He defeated each warrior in turn until eventually he faced Ferdia, a close friend. The pair fought for three days. The battle ended when Cúchulainn used his supernatural javelin to kill Ferdia. While Cúchulainn was in mourning for his friend, Maeve's army stole the bull.

However, the bull was retrieved, and Cúchulainn tied himself to a pillar as he fought Maeve's warriors to the death.

A statute of Cúchulainn in the General Post Office on Dublin's O'Connell Street commemorates the episode.

Little Timmy paid the price for skipping church.

FAMOUS IRISHMEN: RICHARD KIRWAN
(1733-1812)

A chemist, mineralogist, geologist, eccentric and meteorologist, Richard Kirwan became known as the Philosopher of Dublin. Kirwan in fact spent most of his life in Galway, where he married, set up a laboratory and amassed a library.

In later life he became eccentric. He kept a pet eagle on his shoulder and paid his staff to kill flies. He dressed for the outdoors but remained indoors. .

Kirwan was awarded the Copely Medal by the Royal Society in 1782 for his contributions to chemical affinity.

He was the first to describe the titremetric determination of iron with ferrocyanide.

He devised the first quality control test for kelp. Until then, alkali content was assessed by taste and appearance.

Kirwan died in 1812 at the age of 79 from a cold.

68 *Year in the 1900s in which a seat to commemorate the poet Patrick Kavanagh is unveiled alongside Dublin's Grand Canal*

The Gaelic Athletic Association (GAA) was formed at a meeting in Thurles, Co Tipperary, on 1 November 1884. It was to be an association for the 'preservation and cultivation of national pastimes'. The emphasis at the beginning was on athletics, and there was little talk of hurling or football, which were destined to become Ireland's national games and the focus of the GAA.

One of the GAA's founders, Michael Cusack, had been involved with the Dublin Hurling Club, which was formed in 1882. Before it closed, the club played for a while in Phoenix Park. Hurling matches were again held in the park when the GAA was founded.

In 1886, the GAA introduced county committees. These became the units of representation for the new All-Ireland Championship. The local and county organisation still forms the backbone of the GAA today.

The first All-Ireland Championships in hurling and football were organised on a county basis in 1887. Twelve of the 32 counties entered, although only five competed in hurling and eight in football.

In the late nineteenth and early twentieth centuries, the police force – known then as the Royal Irish Constabulary – monitored GAA activities, because many members of the GAA were also involved in the struggle for national independence. On 21 November 1920, in the middle of a match between Tipperary and Dublin, British forces opened fire in Croke Park, headquarters of the GAA. Some 10,000 people were in attendance at the game. At least 12 people, including two players, were killed. The shootings were meant as retaliation for the coordinated killing of 14 British spies by an IRA hit squad earlier that day.

In 1925, 10% of all gate receipts were allocated for grounds development. Loans were advanced for purchase of grounds around the country. This policy was supported by grants from GAA central and provincial boards, and enabled even small parish clubs to own their own premises.

Players at all levels are not paid for participation in games and all are therefore technically amateur sportsmen and women, though a very high level of professionalism prevails.

Fifteen years of planning and development culminated in the opening of a redeveloped stadium at Croke Park in time for the Leinster Football Championship game between Dublin and Meath in June 2002.

The stadium has a capacity of over 82,000 and is one of the most modern in the world. It remains the headquarters of the GAA, a successful association that remains resolutely community-based.

We make out of the quarrel with others, rhetoric, but of our quarrel with ourselves, poetry.

We... are no petty people. We are one of the great stocks of Europe. We are the people of Burke; we are the people of Swift, the people of Emmet, the people of Parnell. We have created most of the modern literature of this country. We have created the best of its political intelligence.

William Butler Yeats, Irish writer, dramatist and poet, from a speech to the Irish senate, 1925

IRISH OBSERVATIONS

Midnight Mass

Christmas-day passed among the peasantry, as it usually passes in Ireland. Friends met before dinner in their own, in their neighbours', in shebeen or in public houses, where they drank, sang, or fought, according to their natural dispositions, or the quantity of liquor they had taken. The festivity of the day might be known by the unusual reek of smoke that danced from each chimney, by the number of persons who crowded the roads, by their brand-new dresses, – for if a young man or country girl can afford a dress at all, they provide it for Christmas, – and by the striking appearance of those who, having drunk a little too much, were staggering home in the purest happiness, singing, stopping their friends, shaking hands with them, or kissing them, without any regard to sex. Many a time might be seen two Irishmen, who had got drunk together, leaving a fair or market, their arms about each other's necks, from whence they only removed them to kiss and hug one another more lovingly. Notwithstanding this, there is nothing more probable than that these identical two will enjoy the luxury of a mutual battle, by way of episode, and again proceed on their way, kissing and hugging as if nothing had happened to interrupt their friendship. All the usual effects of jollity and violence, fun and fighting, love and liquor, were, of course, to be seen, felt, heard, and understood on this day, in a manner much more remarkable than on common occasions; for it may be observed, that the national festivals of the Irish bring out their strongest points of character with peculiar distinctness.

William Carleton, *The Works of William Carleton*, Volume III, Traits and Stories of the Irish Peasantry, Part III

TAXING IRELAND

- Some 95% of adults in Ireland have invested in at least one financial product.
- To oversee matters, the Irish Financial Services Authority was established in 2003, with regulatory responsibilities covering almost 7,000 separate financial institutions.
- Some 50,000 people work in the financial services industry.

IRISH WORDS

The French have *ménage à trois* but the Irish have 'a couple'. When used elsewhere, 'a couple' means two. In Ireland, it can refer to something that goes on for ever.

A couple means a few, and how many is a few depends on the circumstances.

A sin admitted in confession as having been committed a few times could in fact have been occurring regularly.

A few drinks, on the other hand, could presage a long weekend in Galway and several other counties as well.

A few kisses between consenting adults is nice, they say.

THE LATE LATE SHOW

The Late Late Show on RTÉ is the longest-running chat show in the world. Originally conceived as only a short filler programme for the summer schedule of 1962, *The Late Late Show* has gone on to become an Irish institution. Today it is presented by Pat Kenny.

The Late Late Show consists of a two-hour live show broadcast at 9.30pm each Friday from September to May. It is a mixture of interviews with celebrities, local Irish stories, topical debate, music and audience participation.

Gay Byrne, the programme's original presenter and producer, worked on the chat show for 37 years. During his era, *The Late Late Show* began to tackle many of the taboos of Irish society and opened them to national debate.

A frustrated conservative politician, the late Oliver J Flanagan TD, declared that there was no sex in Ireland before *The Late Late Show* arrived. By which he meant people didn't talk about that class of thing. They just did it. A different thing altogether.

BOYLE'S LAW

We all know that Boyle's Law states that at constant temperature, the volume of a gas is inversely proportional to the pressure applied to it. (V x p = constant.)

What is not widely known is that one of his essays is reputed to have inspired the creation of *Gulliver's Travels* by the Dublin-born writer Jonathan Swift.

Although he spent most of his life in Britain, Robert Boyle (1627-1691) was born at Lismore Castle in Co Waterford, the youngest of 14 children.

In his will, Boyle endowed a series of Boyle Lectures, which continue today, 'for proving the Christian religion against notorious infidels'.

His last work, *Free Discourse against Swearing*, published posthumously, was dedicated to his brother, the second Earl of Cork.

Boyle also funded Bible translations into both Irish and Welsh.

He was a founder of the Royal Society in 1661, the same year in which he published *The Sceptical Chymist*.

He invented the air pump and used it to demonstrate that, in a vacuum, sound could not be heard, a feather fell faster, a candle was extinguished, and animals could not survive.

IRISH RIDDLE

How long is a life sentence in Ireland?
Answer on page 153.

PUBLICAN INFORMATION

Closing time in Irish pubs is currently half past midnight on Friday and Saturday nights, and an hour earlier on other nights. The majority of bars open around 11am.

However, there are some bars that open as early as 7.30am (referred to as Early Houses). These are situated beside markets or ports. They were first allowed to open early to cater for manual workers. They are mostly frequented now by night workers relaxing after a shift, partygoers, lost tourists and the needy.

The Celtic languages consist of two divisions, (a) the Gaelic or Irish division, and (b) the Kymric or Welsh division. Between them they comprise (a) Irish, Scotch-Gaelic, Manx, and (b) Welsh, Armorican, and Cornish. All these languages are still alive except Cornish, which died out about a hundred years ago.

Of all these languages Irish is the best preserved, and it is possible to follow its written literature back into the past for some 1,300 years; while much of the most interesting matter has come down to us from pagan times. It has left behind it the longest, the most luminous, and the most consecutive literary track of any of the vernacular languages of Europe, except Greek alone.

For centuries the Irish and their language were regarded by the English as something strange and foreign to Europe. It was not recognised that they had any relationship with the Greeks or Romans, the French, the Germans, or the English. The once well-known statesman, Lord Lyndhurst, in the British parliament denounced the Irish as aliens in religion, in blood, and in language. Bopp, in his great *Comparative Grammar*, refused them recognition as Indo-Europeans, and Pott in 1856 also denied their European connection. It was left for the great Bavarian scholar, John Caspar Zeuss, to prove to the world in his epoch-making *Grammatica Celtica* (published in Latin in 1853) that the Celts were really Indo-Europeans, and that their language was of the highest possible value and interest.

From that day to the present it is safe to say that the value set upon the Irish language and literature has been steadily growing amongst the scholars of the world and, that in the domain of philology, Old Irish now ranks close to Sanscrit for its truly marvellous and complicated scheme of word-forms and inflections, and its whole verbal system.

The oldest alphabet used in Ireland, of which remains exist, appears to have been the Ogam, which is found in numbers of stone inscriptions dating from about the third century of our era on. About 300 such inscriptions have already been found, most of them in the southwest of Ireland, but some also in Scotland and Wales, and even in Devon and Cornwall. Wherever the Irish Gael planted a colony, he seems to have brought his Ogam writing with him.

Douglas Hyde, 'Irish Language and Letters' from *The Glories of Ireland*, 1914

IRISH SAINTS

St Patrick's Day falls on 17 March and honours the national saint. It is used as a day off for those who are observing Lenten sacrifices. Lenten observance resumes on 18 March. It falls in the middle of spring and marks the day when farmers and others traditionally began to plant the potato crop. If St Patrick's Day and Palm Sunday coincide then something unusual in life is expected to happen as a result.

PAY THE TAXMAN

Nobody likes paying taxes, but one development company set a record in 2006 when it settled a tax bill with Revenue Commissioners for €22,169,642.00. Bovale Development's liability included unpaid income tax, corporation tax, VAT, PAYE and PRSI.

The company, owned by brothers Michael and Tom Bailey, paid €12.4m in overdue taxes, and a almost €10m more in interest and penalties under the settlement.

Settlements are not published where a taxpayer has made voluntary disclosure to the Revenue Commissioners. In the three-month period to 31 March 2006, there were 150 settlements published:

- The agreed settlements in these cases totalled €55.55 million
- Eight exceeded €1 million
- Eight exceeded €500,000
- Fifty-four were for amounts exceeding €100,000
- Fifty-nine settlements totalling €12.73 million related to bogus non-resident accounts
- One settlement of €2.75 million related to an Ansbacher account holder.
- Thirty settlements totalling €11.39 million related to Revenue investigations into offshore funds
- One settlement totalling €22.17 million related to the Revenue's tribunal investigations
- Six settlements totalling €930,000 related to the Revenue's single premium insurance product investigation

The published settlements reflected a portion only of all Revenue audits and investigations concluded in that quarter.

The total yield from Revenue audit and investigation programmes in the period was €109.57m. This was a combination of tax, interest and penalties.

The Irish race, to adopt Thierry's language, are full of 'malignant envy' towards the lords of the soil; not because they are rich, but because they have the people so completely in their power, so entirely at their mercy for all that man holds most dear. The tenants feel bitterly when they think that they have no legal right to live on their native land. They have read the history of our dreadful civil wars, famines, and confiscations. They know that by the old law of Ireland, and by custom from times far beyond the reach of authentic history, the clans and tribes of the Celtic people occupied certain districts with which their names are still associated, and that the land was inalienably theirs. Rent or tribute they paid, indeed, to their princes, and if they failed the chiefs came with armed followers and helped themselves, driving away cows, sheep, and horses sufficient to meet their demand, or more if they were unscrupulous, which was 'distress' with a vengeance. But the eviction of the people even for non-payment of rent, and putting other people in their place, were things never heard of among the Irish under their own rulers. The chief had his own mensal lands, as well as his tribute, and these he might forfeit. But as the clansmen could not control his acts, they could never see the justice of being punished for his misdeeds by the confiscation of their lands, and driven from the homes of their ancestors often made doubly sacred by religious associations.

History, moreover, teaches them that, as a matter of fact, the government in the reign of James I – and James himself in repeated proclamations – assured the people who occupied the lands of O'Neill and O'Donnell at the time of their flight that they would be protected in all their rights if they remained quiet and loyal, which they did. Yet they were nearly all removed to make way for the English and Scotch settlers.

James Godkin,
The Land-War in Ireland,
A History for the Times

TALKING MOVIES

Tom Cruise used a decidedly strange Irish accent in the 1992 film *Far and Away*. Irish audiences who saw the film witnessed the transformation of Dublin's Temple Bar into a New York street in midwinter. Seaside scenes were shot on the Dingle peninsula in Kerry. Cruise was in love with his then real-life wife Nicole Kidman's character in the film. They divorced some years afterwards – though this is not thought to have anything to do with Cruise's dodgy accent.

PENALTY POINTS

Penalty points are imposed for driving offences that fall under 36 headings. A driver achieving 12 points is automatically disqualified.

The offences are:

- Dangerous overtaking
- Failure to act in accordance with a garda signal
- Failure to stop before a stop sign line
- Failure to yield right of way at a yield line
- Crossing a continuous white line
- Entry into a hatched marked area of roadway
- Failure to obey traffic lights
- Failure to obey traffic rules at railway level crossing
- Driving a vehicle on a motorway against the flow of traffic
- Driving on the hard shoulder of a motorway
- Driving a HGV or bus on the outside lane of a motorway
- Failure to drive on the left-hand side of the road
- Failure to obey requirements at junctions
- Reversing from minor road onto main road
- Driving on a footpath
- Driving on a cycle track
- Failure to turn left when entering a roundabout
- Driving on a median strip
- Speeding

- Failure to stop for a school warden sign
- Failure to stop when required by a garda
- Failure to leave appropriate distance from the vehicle in front
- Failure to yield
- Driving without reasonable consideration
- Failure to comply with mandatory junction traffic signs
- Failure to comply with prohibitory traffic signs
- Failure to comply with keep left or right signs
- Failure to comply with traffic lane markings
- Illegal entry onto a one-way street
- Driving a vehicle when unfit
- Parking a vehicle in a dangerous position
- Breach of duties at an accident
- Driving without insurance
- Failure to comply with front seat belt requirements
- Failure to comply with rear seat belt requirements for passengers
- Driving carelessly

THE PRIEST THAT NEVER WAS

A plaque commemorating a fictitious priest sat in the wall of Dublin's main river crossing, O'Connell Bridge, for two years without being noticed by council officials. The plaque, which was dedicated to Father Pat Noise, was created as a prank by a pair of anonymous artists.

Installed in 2004, it was not noticed by Dublin City Council officials until May 2006. The inscription claimed that Father Noise had died under suspicious circumstances when his carriage plunged into the Liffey on 10 August 1919.

Many people believed it to be a legitimate plaque, and some went as far as to leave flowers.

It is believed that the hoax is a tribute to the mischievous artists' father, and that 'Father Pat Noise' is a play on the Latin *pater noster*, which translates as 'our father'.

In August 2006, the council said that, because the bridge is a protected structure, no work will be done to remove the plaque until a review of the development of O'Connell Street and the bridge is undertaken. In the meantime, tourists and locals alike have been visiting the plaque.

QUOTE UNQUOTE

I'm troubled, I'm dissatisfied. I'm Irish!
Marianne Moore, American poet and writer

WELL-FED HUNGER STRIKERS

Doubts were expressed about the authenticity of a declared hunger strike in Limerick Prison in the summer of 2006 when it was discovered the strikers may have been making thorough preparations.

According to prison officers, prisoners cleaned out the prison tuck shop during the week before they refused to take food from the canteen. The prisoners bought biscuits, pot noodles and bars of chocolate in copious quantities from the shop.

The 15 convicts later began refusing meals from the canteen. Prison authorities were informed the prisoners were protesting over conditions inside the jail and had made a number of demands, which included more access to the exercise yard, better food from the canteen and a rescheduled gym roster.

A prison spokesman said the prison menu was a standard 28-day one used in all other Irish prisons, and included steak.

*The literary agent thought Oscar Wilde's work
was just too earnest.*

IRISH RIDDLE

Which Irishman was an IRA officer in his youth and later won the
Nobel and Lenin peace prizes and the American Medal of Justice?
Answer on page 153.

DUBLIN PARKS

In the medieval era, St Stephen's Green in Dublin's south city centre
was a marshy common used for public grazing. A water main was laid
in 1880 by Lord Ardilaun (formerly Sir Arthur Edward Guinness) at
his own expense to supply the water features in St Stephen's Green –
and the 300-millimetre pipe is still in service. Ardilaun secured the
passing of an 1877 Act entrusting the green to the Commissioners of
Public Works, allowing access to the public from 1880.

Nineteenth-century Ireland was a place of excess drinking. During this era, as many as 3,000 tents were set up on Sundays in Phoenix Park, west of Dublin, for the sale of whiskey and for gambling. Donnybrook Fair, which was held to the south of the city, was synonymous with drunken debauchery, according to contemporary reports.

So it was not surprising that there should be a backlash against drink.

Father Theobald Mathew began a temperance crusade when he himself took a pledge of total abstinence on 10 April 1838. There had been temperance societies in the past, but these were mainly of Protestant origin, and there was a natural antipathy among the Catholic majority to engage with such movements.

Father Mathew's Total Abstinence Crusade was ecumenical in its origin and remained open to all faiths. It was supported by those non-Catholic organisations that were already attempting to alleviate the vast problems created by alcohol abuse.

Large crowds would gather to hear Father Matthew preach and administer the pledge – a lifelong commitment to abstain from alcohol.

More than 150 years later, non-drinkers who declined the offer of an alcoholic drink on social occasions would be asked if they had taken the pledge,

though Father Mathew had long since passed on.

The crusade was organised along parish lines, with no centralised authority. Each parish set up its own branch of the society. The high point of the crusade seems to have come in 1841, when many temperance societies joined together to parade in Dublin on St Patrick's Day. The different societies marched to a general rendezvous in Phoenix Park while bands played.

The procession was nearly three miles long. A rough estimate of the number of people present on the march was given as 20,000.

The vicious famine that struck in 1845-1849 brought an end to Father Mathew's crusade. Today, his statue stands on O'Connell Street, Dublin.

On 28 December 1898, a Catholic temperance association called the Pioneer Total Abstinence Association of the Sacred Heart was founded by Father James A Cullen in Dublin. During the Association's first year, membership was confined to women. However, men were admitted the following year.

The Pioneer Total Abstinence Association of the Sacred Heart remains in existence to this day, and members, often known as pioneers, may wear a pioneer pin on their clothes to show they are teetotallers – though the practice is not as common as it once was.

For those contemplating marriage in Ireland and who are ordinarily resident in the Irish State, the minimum age at which they may marry is 18 (unless they have a Court Exemption Order).

There is no chance of a Romeo and Juliet running off to a foreign country to marry, and returning to Ireland as a happy pair: the law applies just the same to Irish that marry outside of Ireland.

Even those who are *not* ordinarily resident in the Irish state must be aged more than 18 if they wish to marry someone who *is* ordinarily resident in the Irish state.

A Court Exemption Order allows a marriage to proceed even if one or both parties are under 18. But for a court to grant such an order, applicants have to show there are good reasons for an application, or that the granting of such an exemption order is in the best interests of the parties to the intended marriage.

If either party is under 18 and doesn't have a Court Exemption Order, the marriage will not be recognised under Irish law, and that's that.

There is no longer any requirement for parental consent to a marriage, irrespective of the ages of the parties concerned. This does not necessarily do away with difficulties with in-laws though – these may remain and all parties need to work at extended family relationships.

QUOTE UNQUOTE

The English should give Ireland home rule –
and reserve the motion picture rights.
Will Rogers, American entertainer

GUINNESS NUMBERS

The Guinness Storehouse in Dublin houses:
- More than 7,500 linear metres of records
- Copies of Guinness advertising from 1929 to the present day
- The 9,000-year lease signed by Arthur Guinness on the St James's Gate brewery
- Barley grains nearly 3,500 years old from Tutankhamun's tomb
- Lots of visitors. On Saturday 18 March 2006 there were 4,876 – the highest number recorded in a day.

SAILING AHEAD

The Kerry-born monk St Brendan is credited with sailing to North America in the sixth century – a long time before Columbus managed to bump into an island off that continent in the belief that he had reached India in the fifthteenth century. Brendan is said to have used a currach-type vessel of a kind still made in County Kerry.

In 1976, Tim Severin, a British navigator, embarked on a journey in a currach using the details described by Brendan. His successful voyage proved that a leather currach could have made such a trip.

IRISH OBSERVATIONS

LAND LAW. The entire territory was originally, and always continued to be, the absolute property of the entire clan. Not even the private residence of a clansman, with its *'maighin digona'* = little lawn or precinct of sanctuary, within which himself and his family and property were inviolable, could be sold to an outsider. Private ownership, though rather favoured in the administration of the law, was prevented from becoming general by the fundamental ownership of the clan and the birthright of every free-born clansman to a sufficiency of the land of his native territory for his subsistence. The land officially held as described was not, until the population became numerous, a serious encroachment upon this right. What remained outside this and the residential patches of private land was classified as cultivable and uncultivable. The former was the common property of the clansmen, but was held and used in severalty for the time being, subject to *gabhail-cine* (*gowal-kinneh*) – clan-resumption and redistribution by authority of an assembly of the clan or fine at intervals of from one to three years, according to local customs and circumstances, for the purpose of satisfying the rights of young clansmen and dealing with any land left derelict by death or forfeiture, compensation being paid for any unexhausted improvements. The clansmen, being owners in this limited sense, and the only owners, had no rent to pay. They paid tribute for public purposes, such as the making of roads, to the *flaith* as a public officer, as they were bound to render, or had the privilege of rendering – according to how they regarded it – military service when required, not to the *flaith* as a feudal lord, which he was not, but to the clan, of which the *flaith* was head and representative.

**Laurence Ginnell BL MP,
'Law in Ireland' from
*The Glories of Ireland***

STRAWBERRY FOOL IN APRIL

A radio station's April Fools' day prank led to a complaint being made to the Broadcasting Complaints Commission (BCC) by a listener who thought it was in poor taste. Ms Alexandra Earnshaw reacted to an item on FM 104's Strawberry Alarm Clock broadcast of 1 April 2003.

Listeners heard what was said to be a six-week-old pup being flushed down a toilet to see whether it would sink or float. The pup was supposed to have survived the flushing experiment – but then the programme claimed it jumped out of a third-floor open window to its death. April Fools' prank or not, Earnshaw complained that FM 104 was encouraging cruelty and an irresponsible attitude towards animals.

The station defended itself by repeating that the broadcast was an April Fool's prank, and no more and no less. It said that it was not aware of a single person who had taken the piece seriously.

However, the BCC upheld the complaint. It believed that the piece was in poor taste and the material was particularly unsuitable given the time of the broadcast.

It is inappropriate to make a joke about the suffering of animals, stated the BCC.

A FEW WORDS

English is mostly spoken in Ireland, but in the Irish language this is called *Béarla*. Speaking English is therefore speaking *Béarla*, though that's the Irish word for English.

The Irish word for the Irish language is *Gaeilge* – or, in English, Irish.

To the non-Irish-speaking visitor, Gaelic is the Irish language – though in Ireland, it's not that at all. To the Irish, gaelic is not a language – it is a game of football played by 30 players in two teams with one ball.

The Gaelic Athletic Association (GAA) organises games of gaelic, and sometimes this is done in Irish and sometimes in English, but the referee's decision is final.

There are areas of Ireland where the spoken language has not died out and these are called *Gaeltachts*. Somebody who prefers to live their life through the medium of Irish, yet does not live in a *Gaeltacht* area, is known as a *Gaelgoir*. They can be approached with confidence in either language when seeking directions.

82 *Year in the 1900s when an unsuccessful budget proposal to collect VAT on the sale of children's shoes brought down a coalition government*

She had drawn the guidebook toward her and made good use of it.

'Let us do the literary pilgrimage, certainly, before we leave Ireland, but suppose we begin with something less intellectual. This is the most pugnacious map I ever gazed upon. All the names seem to begin or end with kill, bally, whack, shock, or knock; no wonder the Irish make good soldiers! Suppose we start with a sanguinary trip to the Kill places, so that I can tell any timid Americans I meet in travelling that I have been to Kilmacow and to Kilmacthomas, and am going to-morrow to Kilmore, and the next day to Kilumaule.'

'I think that must have been said before,' I objected.

'It is so obvious that it's not unlikely,' she rejoined; 'then let us simply agree to go afterwards to see all the Bally places from Ballydehob on the south to Ballycastle or Ballymoney on the north, and from Ballynahinch or Ballywilliam on the east to Ballyvaughan or Ballybunnion on the west, and passing through, in transit,

Ballyragget,
Ballysadare,
Ballybrophy,
Ballinasloe,
Ballyhooley,
Ballycumber,
Ballyduff,
Ballynashee,
Ballywhack.

Don't they all sound jolly and grotesque?'

'They do indeed,' we agreed, 'and the plan is quite worthy of you; we can say no more.'

Kate Douglas Wiggin,
Penelope's Irish Experiences

CHRISTMAS CUSTOMS

Children gather holly berries from female holly trees and garland them with ivy to make a traditional Christmas decoration for the home. Male holly trees do not produce berries.

Chimneys in cottages were traditionally cleaned for Christmas fires and Santa Claus's arrival by hauling a prickly bush up and down the chimney's interior with the help of a rope.

Country people attended Christmas fairs to sell country produce and fowl to townspeople. In turn, they purchased town-type goods, including sweets, cakes and toys for Christmas enjoyment.

O'CONNELL BRIDGE

Dubliners love to tell anybody who will listen that the bridge over the Liffey on O'Connell Street is as wide as it is long. In effect it is a square bridge.

Originally designed by James Gandon, the bridge was built between 1794 and 1798, and first named after Lord Carlisle, the then viceroy.

The original O'Connell Bridge had a hump and was much narrower. Gandon designed obelisks and plinths for the four corners. In 1880 it was widened and the hump removed.

Two years later it was renamed after Daniel O'Connell, when the nearby statue in his honour was unveiled.

O'Connell was a lawyer, a lord mayor of Dublin and the architect of Catholic emancipation from penal laws in the nineteenth century. He is also alleged to have been something of a lady's man with an eye for a sporting chance.

IRISH INVENTIONS

Dublin man Aeneas Coffey invented the world's first heat-exchange device in 1830.

Coffey's patent still was a very efficient apparatus that led to many advances in whiskey distilling. This was an important matter for many people.

IRISH SAINTS

Brigid is a Christian saint who was once a pagan goddess, and who was taken over as an object of veneration by the early Christian church. Her day is celebrated on 1 February, the first day of spring. Hoar frost gathered on this day at dawn and rubbed on the head is a sure cure for headache.

The dandelion is known as Brigid's Flower, because it is one of the first wild flowers to appear in spring. In the past, dandelions were used as an ingredient in folk remedies for purifying the blood. These days, it is used to make dandelion coffee or dandelion wine.

Courting couples used to fashion ladders or wheels from rushes and sleep with them beneath their pillows on St Brigid's Eve. They hoped to see their loved one in a dream. If one or both of them did, it meant the couple were destined to marry.

LAND AND PEOPLE IN THE IRISH REPUBLIC

Province	Area (hectares)	Persons per sq km (1996)
Leinster	1,980,066	97
Munster	2,467,410	42
Connacht	1,771,056	24
Ulster (3 counties)	808,776	29
Whole state	7,027,308	52

Notes: There are 2.47 acres in a hectare. The density is as of 1996 and the 2006 census recorded an increase in population, so the density will have changed a little. The area will not.

LOCAL POLITICS

They say that all politics is local – and sometimes it is as important to know when the rubbish bins are to be emptied as it is to know what the national balance of payments might be.

Ireland has a local government system, and citizens make representation through elected representatives.

Local authorities include county councils, city councils and borough or town councils.

At county or city level, there are 29 county councils and five city authorities. These are the main providers of local government services around the country. Within the county council administrative area, there may be a borough or town council area.

Local authorities at all levels are responsible for the representation of local communities and for ensuring that concerns are expressed and needs met.

Local elections are held to elect representatives onto the authority. Local representatives have the power to vote for or against developments that will impact on the local community.

Councils are responsible for the delivery of a wide range of services in their local area. These services include: recreational facilities and amenities; housing; planning; roads; water supply; sewerage; development controls; environmental protection of rivers, lakes and air; and the control of noise.

From 2004, the dual mandate was ended. A councillor must now resign if elected to the national legislature.

The old system allowed TDs or senators to hold a local council seat as well, ensuring their local base was served by them at all levels.

Percentage of guilty pleas entered in criminal cases in Dublin in 2005, 85 according to The Courts Service

IRISH VERSE

Oh, Paddy dear, and did you hear the news that's going round?
The shamrock is by law forbid to grow on Irish ground;
Saint Patrick's Day no more we'll keep, his colours can't be seen,
For there's a cruel law against the wearin' o' the green.
I met with Napper Tandy, and he took me by the hand,
And he said 'How's poor old Ireland, and how does she stand?'
She's the most distressful country that ever yet was seen;
They're hanging men and women there for wearin' o' the green.

Then since the colour we must wear is England's cruel red,
Sure Ireland's sons will ne'er forget the blood that they have shed;
You may take the shamrock from your hand, and cast it in the sod,
But 'twill take root and flourish there, tho' underfoot 'tis trod.
When law can stop the blades of grass from growing as they grow,
And when the leaves in summertime their verdure dare not show,
Then I will change the colour that I wear in my caubeen;
But till that day, please God, I'll stick to wearin' o' the green.

But if at last our colour should be torn from Ireland's heart,
Her sons, with shame and sorrow, from the dear old isle will part;
I've heard whisper of a country that lies beyond the sea,
Where rich and poor stand equal in the light of freedom's day.
Oh, Erin! Must we leave you, driven by a tyrant's hand?
Must we ask a mother's blessing from a strange and distant land?
Where the cruel cross of England shall never more be seen,
And where, please God, we'll live and die still wearin' o' the green.

The Wearin' o' the Green,
Irish street ballad, author unknown, 1798

QUOTE UNQUOTE

*Why should Ireland be treated as a geographical fragment of
England... Ireland is not a geographical fragment, but a nation.*
Charles Stewart Parnell, Anglo-Irish politician

DUBLIN PARKS

Phoenix Park in Dublin is twice the size of New York's Central Park.
Every park in central London would fit into the area covered by
Phoenix Park. The deer herd in the park are descendants of deer
introduced in the mid-seventeenth century.

*Year in the1900s when a referendum to introduce divorce into Ireland
was defeated by 935,842 to 538,729 votes. It was later approved in 1995*

FISHING

Images of tumbling waters might tempt a fisherman to chance his luck with a rod, but there are conditions to be met.

The majority of waters in Ireland are owned either privately or by the state. A fishing permit issued by the owner of the waterway gives the right to fish for varying periods, ranging from a day to a whole season.

The only legal way to catch freshwater fish in Ireland is by rod and line. It is illegal for one person to use more than two rods at a time, and it is illegal to use live fish as bait.

It is also illegal to sell rod-caught salmon or sea trout of over 40 centimetres between 1 January and 31 October.

In addition to permission to fish, a fisherperson must obtain a state fishing licence and tags, and a separate fishing permit to fish for salmon and sea trout. Most game fisheries close for the year on 30 September, with a few exceptions.

KNOCK AIRPORT

The location for Knock Airport in Co Mayo was once described as a 'foggy, boggy place' by an opposition spokesman who said the airport would become a white elephant. Nonetheless, the airport opened for flights on 20 May 1986.

In its early days, weather information was provided by retired Met Éireann personnel. Later, Met staff were relocated to Knock Airport when Claremorris Met Station was automated. Full 24-hour meteorological reports, provided by Met Éireann staff, commenced on 1 April 1996.

Renamed Ireland West Airport, Knock the airport welcomed Mary Croghan from Castlerea as its four millionth passenger on 5 July 2006.

Attracting visitors to the nearby Marian shrine was the underlying idea for the original airport. Under the leadership of Monsignor James Horan, the local parish priest, fundraisers helped raise £3 million to build it.

Two months after the official opening of the airport, Monsignor Horan went on pilgrimage to Lourdes with family and friends – and died unexpectedly. His body was flown from Lourdes to Knock, and was the first funeral to fly into Knock Airport.

When anyone asks me about the Irish character, I say look at the trees. Maimed, stark and misshapen, but ferociously tenacious.
Edna O'Brien, Irish novelist and short story writer

KILLARNEY NATIONAL PARK

When most people think of Killarney, Co Kerry, they think of its famous lakes. The three lakes and the mountains that surround them are all within the Killarney National Park, which was the first such park in Ireland.

Killarney National Park came into being in 1932 when the Muckross Estate – the core of the present-day park – was presented to the nation by Senator Arthur Vincent and Mr and Mrs William Bowers Bourn in memory of Maud Vincent, his late wife and their daughter. UNESCO designated the park as a Biosphere Reserve in 1981.

The park covers more than 10,000 hectares of mountain, moorland, woodland, waterways, parks and gardens, so there is something for everybody to enjoy. The lakes support a large population of trout, as well as an annual run of salmon, and angling is a popular pastime.

The well-preserved remains at Inisfallen Abbey are from a monastic settlement founded in the seventh century and inhabited until the fourteenth century. They stand on an island in Lough Leane, the largest of the three lakes. The park also includes Muckross Traditional Farming Project, a re-creation of life in rural Ireland before the advent of electricity.

But not all human innovation has been for the good of the area. Killarney has suffered from interference with the local terrain, including the uncontrollable spread of the common rhododendron, which was introduced into the park in the late nineteenth century.

Another alien invader has been the American mink, which was introduced by fur farmers and escaped into the wild. Mink are now firmly established in the park alongside the native otter. Japanese sika deer also overgraze woodlands, and they pose a threat to the genetic integrity of the native red deer.

A number of rangers are employed to facilitate the day-to-day running of the park, and they undertake projects aimed at assisting the survival of its wild nature.

OLD PICTURE, NEW CAPTION

*Mary had underestimated how long it would take
to paddle to England.*

IRISH RIDDLE

Which letters do not appear in the 18-letter
Irish language alphabet?
Answer on page 153.

ROAD SPEED LIMITS

Town and city speed limits 50kph
National road speed limits. 100kph
Regional and local speed limits 80kph
Motorway speed limits 120kph

Ordinary speed limits

Double-deck vehicles. 65kph
Buses and coaches 80kph
(with accommodation for more than eight passengers)
Towing vehicles. 80kph
Trucks 80kph
(with a design gross weight of more than 3,500 kilograms)

Fragments of an ancient manuscript, possibly more than 1,000 years old, were uncovered in a Midlands bog in the summer of 2006. Text on the vellum manuscript comes from Psalm 83 of the old Latin translation of the Bible, known as the Vulgate, which corresponds to Psalm 84 of the much later King James version.

Archaeologists said the accidental discovery of an ancient book of psalms by a bulldozer driver was a miracle. It could easily have been destroyed or ended up as part of a peat briquette destined for a domestic fire.

The 20-page Psalter, or Book of Psalms, has been dated to between 800-1000AD. It was immediately placed in safekeeping in the National Museum in Dublin, prior to painstaking cleaning and examination. It will go on display to the public in the future.

A possible explanation for the Psalter's presence in a bog is that it may have been discarded by a monastery raider who regarded it as worthless. The Psalter is the first major find in an Irish bog for 200 years.

BANNING MOVIES

Film censorship began in Ireland with the introduction of the Censorship of Films Act in 1923. All nine subsequent censors have been male. There is only ever a single censor appointed, though there is a nine-person appeal board to which representations can be made.

According to the Act, films considered to be indecent, obscene or blasphemous, or that may affect public morality, were to be banned or cut. Successive censors interpreted the law in their own ways and imposed their own ethical universe on the cinema-going public.

A subsequent problem was that all films passed were given a general certificate and supposed to be suitable for a child to watch.

Some 2,500 theatrical films have been banned while about 11,000 have been cut – many before 1965, when classification of certificates by viewer's age was introduced.

Times have moved on and, today, few films are either banned or cut – with the exception of pornography. Certificates now have a parental guidance element helping a parent decide whether a film is suitable for viewing by their children.

This is a major change from the previous situation whereby one man decided what was appropriate for everyone to view.

EUROVISION

Ireland's winning streak in the Eurovision Song Contest began with Dana's entry in the 1970 competition in Amsterdam. She sang 'All Kinds of Everything', composed by Derry Lindsay and Jackie Smith.

FRANK O'CONNOR INTERNATIONAL SHORT STORY AWARD

At €35,000, the Frank O'Connor International Short Story Award is the largest prize of its type in the world. Entries have to be original collections of short stories published in English, anywhere in the world, for the first time in a given year.

In 2005, the inaugural prize went to Chinese author Yiyun Li for her debut collection of short stories, *A Thousand Years of Good Prayers*. Li grew up in Beijing and moved to the United States in 1996. She says she taught herself to write by reading the work of Cork-born author William Trevor, who was also long-listed for the prize.

Originally the prize was for €50,000, to be awarded every two years, but such was its success that it has already been upgraded to an annual €35,000 prize funded by Cork City Council.

The Munster Literature Centre, organisers of the competition, pay for hotel and economy travel expenses of short-listed authors who attend the ceremony.

QUOTE UNQUOTE

You cannot conquer Ireland. You cannot extinguish the Irish passion for freedom. If our deed has not been sufficient to win freedom, then our children will win it by a better deed.
Padraig Pearse, leader of the Easter Rising, 1916

RELICS

The relics of the seventeenth-century French Jesuit who promoted the Sacred Heart of Jesus went on tour around Ireland in the summer of 2006. The bones of St Claude de la Colombiere completed a five-week journey through all 26 Catholic dioceses. This was the only time in 300 years that his relics left the shrine of Paray-le-Monial in France.

Julie found that her diet of potatoes didn't quite agree with her.

IRISH OBSERVATIONS

A Short View of the State of Ireland

Ireland is the only Kingdom I ever heard or read of, either in ancient or modern story, which was denied the liberty of exporting their native commodities and manufactures wherever they pleased, except to countries at war with their own Prince or State, yet this by the superiority of mere power is refused us in the most momentous parts of commerce, besides an Act of Navigation to which we never consented, pinned down upon us, and rigorously executed, and a thousand other unexampled circumstances as grievous as they are invidious to mention. To go unto the rest.

It is too well known that we are forced to obey some laws we never consented to, which is a condition I must not call by its true uncontroverted name for fear of my Lord Chief Justice Whitshed's ghost with his *Libertas et natale solum*, written as a motto on his coach, as it stood at the door of the court, while he was perjuring himself to betray both. Thus, we are in the condition of patients who have physic sent them by doctors at a distance, strangers to their constitution, and the nature of their disease: And thus, we are forced to pay five hundred *per cent* to divide our properties, in all which we have likewise the honour to be distinguished from the whole race of mankind.

Jonathan Swift, *The Prose Works of Jonathan Swift DD,*
Historical and Political Tracts – Irish

A census taken in 2006 found that the population of Ireland had risen to its highest level since 1861. The population had also increased by 318,000 since the previous census, which was taken in 2002.

The preliminary total for the population enumerated on census night (23 April 2006) was 4,234,925 persons, compared with 3,917,203 in April 2002 – and this figure represented an increase of 8.1% in four years, or 2% per annum, according to the Central Statistics Office (CSO).

Net migration into Ireland was a dominant factor in the increase, a pattern that reversed a long trend of net emigration. On average, 46,000 more immigrants arrived than emigrants left each year during the 2002-2006 period. The annual excess of births over deaths was 33,000.

From a 10-year perspective, Ireland's population increased at an annual average rate of 1.6% between 1996 and 2006 – the largest population growth rate in the EU. The only other countries to record population growth rates in excess of 1% were Cyprus (1.5%) and Luxembourg (1.2%).

The spread of the Greater Dublin area into the surrounding counties was reflected in growth in those counties' populations. The populations of Fingal (up by 43,400) and Meath (up by 28,616) both increased by more than a fifth between 2002 and 2006. Along with Kildare (22,131), these areas together accounted for 30% of the national increase.

Other Leinster counties that showed large increases were Laois (14%), Wexford (12.9%), Offaly (10.9%), Westmeath (10.5%) and Wicklow (10.2%).

Reflecting high house prices in Dublin, there was a relatively modest increase of just 20,000 in the rest of the capital and, as a consequence, the overall population grew by just 5.6% – which is considerably less than the 8.1% increase for the state as a whole.

The population of Co Leitrim grew by almost 12% between 2002 and 2006. This followed a modest increase of 3% between 1996 and 2002, which was considered remarkable in itself, in that it occurred after a continuous decline in the county's population over the previous century and a half.

Between 2002 and 2006, only six of the 34 administrative districts in the Republic of Ireland experienced net outward migration. These were the cities of Limerick, Cork, Waterford and Dublin, along with Dublin South and Dún Laoghaire-Rathdown.

According to the CSO, this was due to a combination of factors, including adult children leaving the family home and urban renewal schemes.

*Year in the 1900s in which Irish laws were amended to make 93
contraceptives more freely available to everybody*

HOMING DOGS

In 2006, Louth County Council won an award for public service excellence for its animal compound. The facility has 16 individual kennels and four large stables.

The compound has a wind turbine to supply 60% of its electrical needs from renewable energy. It embraces the latest in information technology, and has a wireless broadband link with county hall and town councils in Dundalk and Drogheda.

Members of the public can go online to view still pictures of animals in the pound and some details of their health and history. The council says this facilitates 're-homing', and allows worried dog owners to check for lost dogs at any time.

Indeed, the project has improved the re-homing rate from 20% to more than 60% and resulted in a radical reduction in the number of dogs that need to be put to sleep.

WHERE'S THE MONEY?

It seems that Irish people had so much disposable income in the new millennium that some €11 billion in cash disappeared each year. That is, few could recall what they spent the money on.

Each adult got through some €66.59 in petty cash each week – or €3,460 per year.

Research commissioned by Visa Europe in 2006 as part of a lifestyle study revealed that almost 25% of their mortgage payment could have been paid by the cash people lost track of each year.

Unrecollected spending included money spent on a night out, on groceries and clothes. Shopping in the sales, or when out with family, was also likely to result in financial moments that were to be forgotten later.

Women were more likely to spend vaguely, though not by much. Women averaged €69 a week to a men's slightly more modest €63.

Men were more likely to lose track while shopping online, going for a night out, or buying music.

Not surprisingly, Visa Ireland pointed out that the use of a credit card would help people keep a proper track of where their money went. The money would still get spent though!

LOVE ME DEARLY

One of the earliest mythological love affairs concerned Grainne, the wife-to-be of Fionn MacCumhaill, the most powerful man in Ireland at the time. At her wedding feast, Grainne ran off with the handsome Diarmuid after his magic made her fall hopelessly in love with him. The lovers were found by Fionn, but Diarmuid gave Grainne a cape of invisibility and they escaped. Eventually, Aengus, the god of poets, appeared to Fionn to plead the lovers' case and all were reconciled.

IRISH RIDDLE

Where was the first Jewish temple built in Ireland?
Answer on page 153.

IRISH VERSE

The sounds of Ireland,
that restless whispering
you never get away
from, seeping out of
low bushes and grass,
heatherbells and fern,
wrinkling bog pools,
scraping tree branches,
light hunting cloud,
sound hounding sight,
a hand ceaselessly
combing and stroking
the landscape, till
the valley gleams
like the pile upon
a mountain pony's coat

John Montague, *Windharp*

IRISH INVENTIONS

Dublin-born innovator Lucien Bull pioneered high-speed photography. Strangely enough, he did so to view images in slow motion. In 1938, Bull also patented an improved version of the electrocardiogram (ECG), a test that records the electrical activity of the heart.

SMASHING TRUCKS

Millions of euro were spent by Dublin City Council to build a port tunnel nearby with a clearance of 4.65 metres.

Complaining about the tunnel's low height, the Irish Road Transport Association pointed out that every motorway bridge constructed in the UK or Ireland in the past 30 years had a height clearance of five metres or more.

Nonetheless, Transport Minister Martin Cullen gave the project his blessing.

WHO'S IN CHARGE?

An Garda Síochána (Guardians of the Peace) is the national police force in the Republic of Ireland. One police officer is usually referred to as a Garda. Its command structure is as follows:

Commissioner
Deputy Commissioners
Assistant Commissioners
Chief Superintendents
Inspectors
Sergeants
Gardaí

IRISH LITERARY REVIVAL

Ireland has a long tradition of storytelling and writing, but many writers fail to see their work in print for one reason or another.

While it may be difficult for some writers to be published in the first place, many others – especially poets – experience the frustration of seeing their work go out of print. So, with such readers and writers in mind, a free, virtual library was launched in 2006.

Every previously published and currently unavailable Irish book, or book of Irish interest, is eligible for consideration, be it an anthology of poetry, a novel, a collection of short stories, a play or a work of non-fiction.

All work on the site is released under a Creative Commons Licence, so that authors retain their copyright while allowing the texts to be downloaded.

A writer sends an electronic copy of their eligible book, with details of its history and status, to the site. If approved, the librarians upload it.

The website can be visited at: www.irishliteraryrevival.com.

BOG OF ALLEN

The Bog of Allen is the largest complex of raised bog in Ireland. It covers an area of 115,080 hectares located in nine counties across the Midlands.

It is a wetland system that took 10,000 years to form and is made from peat. More than 90% of it has been lost to drainage and peat mining during the last 400 years. Habitats in the bog include raised bog, heathland, woodland, wild flower grassland, lake, fen, swamp and canal.

An Irish Peatland Conservation Council survey identified 17 wildlife habitats and 185 species of plant and animal in the Bog of Allen area.

During its formation, peat accumulated and filled a lake basin to create a fen. Sphagnum moss invaded the peatland, changing the fen into an acid bog. It became raised above the level of the surrounding land and is fed by rainwater.

Remains of prehistoric settlements, medieval leather shoes, early Christian bog roads, bog butter, coins, dugout wooden canoes and even a 10,000-year-old skeleton of a great Irish elk have all been found preserved in the bog.

TAXING IRELAND

Value Added Tax (VAT) was introduced in Ireland in 1972. It replaced wholesale and turnover taxes.

VAT is a general sales tax applied at all stages of production and distribution to the supply of taxable goods and services.

The rates are currently zero, 4.8%, 13.5% and 21%.

A SONG FOR IRELAND

Dubliner Bob Geldof co-wrote 'Do they know its Christmas?' with Midge Ure in 1984 specifically to raise money for Ethiopian famine relief. The massive follow-up Live Aid concert in 1985 raised cash for the same cause.

HOW TO VOTE

● Proportional representation is the system of voting used in all Irish elections. Voters cast a single transferable vote in multi-seat constituencies. They indicate first and subsequent choices of candidates on the ballot paper. Voters indicate a first choice by writing '1' opposite the first choice and '2' opposite a second choice, and so on.

● Using this system, a returning officer is asked to transfer a vote to the second choice candidate if the first choice is either elected with a surplus of votes over the quota or eliminated. If a second choice is elected or eliminated, the vote is transferred to the third choice, and so on.

● The Total Valid Poll is the total number of votes minus the number of spoiled papers.

● A quota is calculated by dividing the Total Valid Poll by one more than the number of seats to be filled, ignoring any remainder, and then adding one vote. For example, in a Dáil election in a four-seat constituency with 50,000 votes cast, the calculation is: 50,000 divided by five (that is four plus one) equals 10,000; 10,000 plus one is 10,001. This is the quota of votes to be reached by the candidates for election.

IRISH WEATHER

Ireland's position in northwestern Europe, close to the path of Atlantic low pressure systems, means that it tends to experience humid, cloudy airflows for much of the time.

In the century between 1881 and 1980, the year 1887 had the sunniest summer, according to measurements made at Phoenix Park in Dublin.

The dullest summer in that period came in 1980. The summer of 1887 was measured as twice as sunny as that of 1980 – so older people who used to claim summers were sunnier in their childhood may well have been right.

The highest temperature recorded since records began in Ireland was 33.3°C at Kilkenny Castle on 26 June 1887.

Mid-July 2006 saw temperatures rise to around 30°C in Kilkenny during a heatwave. However, the nineteenth-century record remained unbroken.

A Glance at the Future Destiny of Ireland

There is no other phrase which so well expresses the character of Irish political history, as the single word, extraordinary. Singular, indeed, have been the fortunes of the Hibernian Celts, and their descendants. Ireland was old when Christianity exiled the Druids from their sacrificial forests; her commerce was known at Rome, but not her captives; Tyre and Sidon had bartered with her, before Romulus and his brother had forsaken Alba. Her military fame, at an early time, was equally celebrated; her soldiers trampled down the Roman fortifications, and were about to scale the Alps, when an arrow of lightning, launched from the thunder-cloud above, struck down Dathy, their daring general – yet a handful of needy Normans overran her sea-coast, and, profiting by the jealousies of rival chiefs, seized on the pleasant plains of Leinster. Seven hundred years of slavery have scarcely cured them of that besetting sin. Early in her Christian ages, when Europe was buried in barbarism, letters and science found a shelter amidst her glens, where like a conservatory, those precious plants were screened from inclemency of that Gothic winter, which had set in on all the cities and states of the continent. When literature 'revived' abroad, in the latter part of the sixteenth century, penal laws and Protestantism had commenced the work of devastation in Ireland; then, what the Vandals had done for Rome, and the Saracens for Spain, Henry and Elizabeth performed for Ireland. With the accession of the Guelphs this was completed; and ignorance and the Reformation were established by law together. This eccentric destiny clung to the land even later; in the history of the Stuart war in Ireland, it is strangely exemplified. The revolution of 1688 gave new security to the liberties of the empire, but refastened the fetters of Ireland. Her soldiers went abroad to win glory in a foreign service; her scholars were proscribed and incarcerated; and while the reign of Anne is the brightest era in English literary history, it becomes the darkest in that of Ireland. In 1798, the Presbyterians and Catholics first combined to save the constitution, and enlarge its pale so as to take in all creeds; but again a blight came o'er their councils – and from willing comrades in danger, they were artfully turned into enemies, underrating and suspecting each other.

Thomas D'Arcy McGee,
Historical Sketches of
O'Connell and his Friends,
with a Glance at the Future
Destiny of Ireland

QUOTE UNQUOTE

There is an Irish way of paying compliments as though they were irresistible truths, which makes what would otherwise be an impertinence delightful.
Katherine Tynan Hinkson, Irish poet and novelist

AN IRISH FIRST

Stephen Roche was the first Irishman to win the Tour de France and the World Professional Road Championship in 1987. He was the second rider in history to win the Giro d'Italia, Tour de France and the World Professional Championship in the same year.

NO TAILS IN IRELAND

There are no 'tails' on coins in Ireland. Instead of the cry of 'heads or tails' heard in other countries, before a coin is tossed an Irish person will ask whether you would like to bet on heads or harps.

In 1927, when coins for the newly independent state were introduced, the poet and senator William Butler Yeats suggested Irish coins should bear illustrations of a variety of creatures. Subsequent designs included an Irish hare, a stallion, a salmon and a hen. This side was known as 'heads'.

The flip side showed the Celtic harp, a traditional symbol of Ireland, decorated with the year of issue and the word *Éire* – the Irish word for Ireland. This side was known as 'harps'. The harp shown was designed by Jarlath Hayes.

With the advent of the euro, Irish coins were redesigned in 2002 to show maps of Europe and to symbolise the unity of the European Union. However the harp remains on one side.

In 2006, the Central Bank issued a proof coin set for Ireland, the first of its type ever to go on sale. The set was limited to only 5,000 pieces for issue worldwide, and sold out in a matter of four days.

The set was valued at €60 by the bank.

IRISH UNDERSTATEMENT

'A soft day' refers to a rainy day with a particular soft drizzle, and an overcast sky, but relatively bright. You still get soaked, however, and a 'sun shower' does not dry you at the same time as it drenches you.

IRISH AUTHORS

Robert Erskine Childers was the author of the 1903 spy novel, *The Riddle of the Sands*. The book is the retelling of a yachting expedition around German waters in the early twentieth century, combined with an adventurous spy story. It was one of the early invasion-warning novels that predicted war with Germany and called for Britain to make preparations.

Childers was a Londoner by birth. He moved to Dublin to become involved in the struggle against British rule. In 1919 he was director of publicity for the first Irish parliament.

Childers joined the anti-treaty side in the Irish Civil War and was executed by opposing forces. He was aged 52.

His son Erskine Hamilton Childers served as the fourth president of Ireland from 1973 until his death in office the following year.

INTERNATIONAL IMPAC AWARD

When, in 2006, Colm Tóibín was declared the winner of the International IMPAC Dublin Literary Award for *The Master*, he was the first Irish writer to win the award in its 11-year history.

At €100,000, the award is the world's richest literary prize for a single work of fiction published in English. Nominations are by public libraries. *The Master* was chosen by an international panel of judges, having been nominated by 17 libraries worldwide.

The 10 short-listed titles in 2006 included three Irish authors and were selected from 132 novels, nominated by 180 libraries from 124 cities in 43 countries. Thirty-two titles were in translation, covering 15 non-English languages.

An original purse of IR£100,000 was reduced to €100,000 on the changeover to the euro in 2002. The award's value is now IR£78,760 in pre-euro currency.

IMPAC, the sponsor, is a productivity improvement company operating in more than 50 countries.

The award is administered by Dublin City Public Libraries. If a novel in translation wins, 75% of the award goes to the author and 25% to the translator.

IRISH RIDDLE

Which president of Ireland was born in the United States?
Answer on page 153.

POLITICAL PARTIES IN DÁIL EIREANN

166 deputies (TDs) were returned in 42 constituencies in the 2002 General Election:

Fianna Fáil *81*
Fine Gael *31*
Labour *21*
Progressive Democrats *8*
Green Party *6*
Sinn Féin *5*
Socialist Party *1*
Others *13*

Fianna Fáil and the Progressive Democrats formed a government

DUBLIN'S MANSION HOUSE

In the eighteenth century, the yearly rent for the Lord Mayor of Dublin's official residence, Mansion House, was 40 shillings and a loaf of double-refined sugar weighing six pounds each Christmas.

Dublin's mayor still lives in Mansion House, which is on Dawson Street. The building was also the venue for the first session of an Irish parliament in the twentieth century.

The Mansion House was built in 1710 by the merchant and property developer Joshua Dawson, after whom Dawson Street is named.

On 25 April 1715, the City Corporation purchased the house at a cost of £3,500. In return, Dawson agreed to build on an extra room, which could be used for civic receptions – the famous Oak Room.

Sinn Féin members elected in the 1918 Westminster election refused to take up their seats in London. They subsequently set up the first Dáil Éireann (parliament) at Mansion House.

The Dáil Éireann was elected on 18 December 1918 and met in the Round Room on 21 January 1919, on which date the First Ministry assumed office. It lasted for 892 days.

However, the assembly was not recognised or welcomed by the British, and it prompted the War of Independence, which resulted in independence for 26 counties out of 32, and the establishment of Northern Ireland following the partition of the country in 1922.

The FM frequency once used by Q102 a pirate radio station in Dublin and now used by Dublin's Q102 a respected licenced station

The Duke of Wellington, who routed Napoleon at Waterloo and gave his name to the wellie, famously declared that being born in a stable did not make you a horse. Avowedly Anglo-Irish, he was referring to his Irish birth. To prove his point, Wellington became British prime minister when he was 58 years old.

Nonetheless, Dublin honoured him by giving his name to a number of public places.

Wellington Quay was the last of Liffey quay to be constructed and was named in honour of the good Arthur Wellesley, First Duke of Wellington, following his victory over Napoleon. It flanks Temple Bar.

The nearby Ha'penny Bridge was named Wellington Bridge in the Duke's honour when it opened in 1816 as a pedestrian toll bridge.

It cost a ha'penny to cross the river, which is why it is now known as Ha'penny Bridge. Payment is no longer necessary to cross the bridge.

The Wellington Monument in Phoenix Park was raised by public subscription. Work on the granite monument began in 1817, while Wellington was alive, and was only completed in 1861, nine years after his death.

Had it not been for a shortage of funds, it would have been 4.5 metres taller than it is.

Nevertheless, at 67 metres high, the monument was the world's tallest obelisk for several years. For many years after that, it came second only to the Washington Memorial, which is 169 metres.

Each of the Wellington Monument's four sides features bronze plaques cast from cannons captured at the Battle of Waterloo in 1815.

The inscription on the city-facing side reads:

Asia and Europe, saved by thee, proclaim
Invincible in war thy deathless name,
Now round thy brow the civic oak we twine
That every earthly glory may be thine.

A plan to install a statue of Wellington, mounted on a horse, beside his monument was eventually abandoned due to lack of funds.

AN OLDIE BUT A GOODIE

Dubliner David Tyndall completed a helicopter solo flight at the age of 82 over Co Kildare on 30 July 1999. He had his first flying lesson in 1965 in a fixed-wing aircraft. The octogenarian practised for his record attempt for two years after his wife, Moll, gave him a birthday gift of helicopter lessons.

Age at which teacher Patrick Greene received an honorary degree at 103 NUI Galway, for contributions to Irish education and collecting of folklore

Brehon Law was a system of arbitration and justice that was used in Ireland from the seventh century onwards and not fully supplanted across Ireland until as late as the seventeenth century, when English law took over.

Brehon Laws grew from practice and experience. For many years they remained unwritten, but they were eventually recorded, principally in the seventh century.

The system was administered by Brehons, who were the successors of the Celtic druids. They acted as arbiters rather than judges and, in most cases, they prescribed restitution rather than punishment for wrongdoing.

The king's rights as ruler were acknowledged, but his duties to his people were also defined.

Brehon Law recognised divorce and equal rights for men and women. Women held a place of respect in Celtic society and were accorded their entitlements under the law. They were rulers in their own right and led their troops into battle. They could be druids, poets, physicians, sages, and lawgivers as a matter of course.

Upon marriage, a woman was a partner with, and not the property of, her husband. She remained the sole owner of property that had been hers prior to marriage. If the couple divorced, she retained what was hers, and an agreement was reached regarding any property she jointly owned with her former husband.

English rule was extended to Ireland in 1210 by the English Crown, but Brehon Law survived until the seventeenth century, when it was finally replaced by English Common Law.

Capital punishment was not among the range of penalties used by the Brehons. Cases of homicide or bodily injury were punishable by means of a fine, the exact amount determined by a scale.

In general criminal law, offences and penalties were defined in great detail, so defending or aggrieved parties knew what to expect when they faced a hearing.

Curiously, given that Ireland was to develop into a Roman Catholic country that paid great attention to the Vatican's rules for life, the first encroachment on Brehon Law came at the instigation of Rome in 1155, when Pope Adrian IV issued a papal bull endorsing Henry II's plan to conquer Ireland.

The Anglo-Normans were successful in imposing their will on the Irish, but both sides inter-married through the generations, and Brehon Law came back into widespread use.

In the succeeding centuries, English law was confined to an area known as the Pale, made up of Dublin and a small part of the east coast. Beyond the Pale, Brehon Law continued to be applied by the native Irish.

The end of Brehon Law came in 1603, when Ireland was divided into counties and English law was finally administered throughout the country.

OLD PICTURE, NEW CAPTION

*Trying to capture the beauty of the Irish landscape nearly
drove Paul Henry to distraction.*

QUOTE UNQUOTE

*When the Irishman is found outside of Ireland in another
environment, he very often becomes a respected man. The economic
and intellectual conditions that prevail in his own country do not
permit the development of individuality. No one who has any
self-respect stays in Ireland, but flees afar as though from a country
that has undergone the visitation of an angered Jove.*

Ireland is the sow that eats her own farrow.

Joyce James, novelist

KIDNAPPING

Kidnapping for ransom would appear to be a straightforward proposition for the kidnappers, but when several high-profile kidnappings occurred in the 1970s and 1980s, the Irish state responded by searching every house in the country with a mixture of *gardaí* and soldiers. In the main, people waived their right to have a search warrant issued for a search of their home.

Dr Tiede Herrema was kidnapped by IRA members Eddie Gallagher and Marion Coyle on 3 October 1975. Herrema was head of the Dutch-owned Ferenka factory in Limerick at the time. He was released after 27 days when he and his captors were traced to a house in Monasterevin, Co Kildare. Gallagher and Coyle surrendered after a two-week siege. They were sentenced to 25 years and 20 years in prison respectively.

The kidnapping of supermarket boss Don Tidey led to a nationwide search and culminated in a shoot-out at Derrada Wood, Co Leitrim, in December 1983. A trainee *garda*, Gary Sheehan, and a soldier, Private Patrick Kelly, were killed during the rescue of Tidey.

In October 1987, John O'Grady, a 38-year-old Dublin dentist, was kidnapped in what was taken to be a case of mistaken identity. Dr Austin Darragh, the father-in-law of O'Grady, used to live in the dentist's Cabinteely house, and may have been the target of the paramilitary gang, which was led by Dessie O'Hare. During captivity, the kidnap victim had two fingers amputated by the gang with a hammer and chisel without anaesthetic. O'Grady escaped during a shoot-out between *gardaí* and the kidnappers in a Dublin housing estate. O'Hare was later sentenced to 40 years.

IRISH RIDDLE

Which American was hanged in Britain and buried in Galway?
Answer on page 153.

RECORD BREAKERS

Irishman Robbie Bolger reached a speed of 169.19kph while performing a handlebar wheelie on the set of *Guinness World Records* at Temora Aerodrome, New South Wales, Australia on 29 March 2005. He was riding a Suzuki GSX-R1000.

FARMERS AND LANDOWNERS

Tenant farmers were farmers who held their land under a landlord to whom they paid rent. Under penal laws that discriminated against Catholics and until emancipation was achieved in 1829, just 5% of Catholics owned land. The landowners were predominantly Protestant and absent. Their properties and tenants were administered by land agents.

Small farmers owned their own small parcels of land. However, under eighteenth-century penal laws, on death the land of those Catholic small farmers was divided up among male children, resulting in holdings of an ever decreasing size. Catholics were not allowed to own a horse worth more than £5, an essential item for farming in an era before mechanisation.

In the twenty-first century, many farmers effectively ceased full-time farming. Under EU schemes to manage production across Europe, they received regular cheques from Brussels. As a consequence, a number of farmers became part-timers with day jobs to attend to.

GUINNESS RECORDS

As is the case with most things to do with Guinness, the company's famous compendium of world records originated in Ireland. The story goes that while staying at Castlebridge House in Co Wexford as part of a shooting party in the 1950s, Sir Hugh Beaver, managing director of Guinness, was involved in a dispute over whether the golden plover was Europe's fastest game bird. Another argument arose over whether grouse were faster than golden plover.

Beaver realised that such questions could arise in pubs, and a book providing answers would be of use to licencees.

Twins Norris and Ross McWhirter were commissioned to compile *The Guinness Book of Records* and the first copy, a 198-page tome, was bound on 27 August 1955.

The Guinness Book of Records' English edition is currently distributed in 70 different countries worldwide, while a further 22 editions are available in translation.

Ross McWhirter was an outspoken critic of the IRA. He was shot dead in 1975 by the group after offering a £50,000 reward for information leading to the capture of IRA bombers in England.

IRISH INVENTIONS

Cork-born Vincent Barry (1908-1975) and his team were delighted to discover a compound, B663, that ultimately led to a treatment for leprosy. However, the team was working on a cure for tuberculosis at the time. Leprosy is not a common ailment in Ireland, though a good few people suffer from TB.

SAM THE MAN

Dubliner and Nobel laureate Samuel Beckett may be feted and famous now – but it was not always thus. One little-known literary link is that, in Paris in 1932, he took up a job as secretary to a fellow Dubliner, James Joyce. His duties included helping to research the work that would eventually become Joyce's famous novel *Finnegans Wake*.

Beckett's own novel *Murphy* was rejected by more than 40 publishers before finding favour in 1938. The same year the 32-year old Beckett was stabbed by a pimp on a Paris street and almost died. He later married Suzanne Deschevaux-Dumesnil who came across him on the ground on that occasion.

When the Nazi occupation of France began in 1940, Beckett and his wife became active in a local intelligence network known as 'Gloria'. His group was awarded the Croix de Guerre in 1945.

Another of Beckett's claims to fame is that he wrote the world's shortest play, *Breath*, which is 30 seconds long. His more famous work, *Waiting for Godot,* is somewhat longer and is regularly performed all over the world.

The play features two men, Vladimir and Estragon, who wait on a lonely country road for an appointment with Godot. After a while Pozzo enters, leading Lucky on a rope. They talk. Godot fails to arrive. That's it.

It was first presented in French as *En Attendant Godot* at the Theatre de Babylone, 38 Boulevard Raspail, Paris, on 5 January 1953. The English language premiere, directed by Peter Hall, took place at the Arts Theatre Club, London, on 3 August 1955.

Ever shy of personal publicity, when Beckett was awarded a Nobel prize for literature in 1969, he declined to travel to Stockholm to personally receive the accolade.

Samuel Beckett died on 22 December 1989, just five months after his wife had passed away. He is buried in Paris.

QUOTE UNQUOTE

In Ireland, the inevitable never happens and the unexpected constantly occurs.
Sir John Pentland Mahaffey, Irish scholar

SMASHING TRUCKS

The most struck railway bridge in Ireland is the East Wall Road Bridge, a main access route to Dublin Port.

In 2003, exasperated rail engineers raised its height from 4.65 metres to 5.3 metres in response to truck accidents.

IRISH CITIES

City charters were granted by the British monarch of the day and detailed the rights and privileges to be enjoyed by the citizens under the charter. The Republic now has no monarch, obviously.

REPUBLIC OF IRELAND
Dublin, *charter granted 1192*
Cork, *charter granted 1318*
Galway, *charter granted 1484*
Kilkenny, *charter granted 1609*
Limerick, *charter granted 1179*
Waterford, *charter granted 1205*

NORTHERN IRELAND
Belfast, Co Antrim and Co Down,
charter granted 1613
Derry, Co Derry, *charter granted 1613*
Armagh, Co Armagh, *charter granted 1994*
Newry, Co Down, *charter granted 2002*
Lisburn, Co Antrim and Co Down, *charter granted 2002*

IRISH UNDERSTATEMENT

'His nerves are at him' could refer to a lunatic on the rampage or a man sitting in a field of daisies wondering how a daisy chain works.

THE EASTER PROCLAMATION

The Easter Proclamation, read by Pádraig Pearse outside the General Post Office, Dublin, at the start of the Easter Rising on 24 April 1916.

The Provisional Government of the Irish Republic to the People of Ireland

IRISHMEN AND IRISH-WOMEN: In the name of God and of the dead generations from which she receives her old tradition of nationhood, Ireland, through us, summons her children to her flag and strikes for her freedom.

Having organised and trained her manhood through her secret revolutionary organisation, the Irish Republican Brotherhood, and through her open military organisations, the Irish Volunteers and the Irish Citizen Army, having patiently perfected her discipline, having resolutely waited for the right moment to reveal itself, she now seizes that moment, and, supported by her exiled children in America and by gallant allies in Europe, but relying in the first on her own strength, she strikes in full confidence of victory.

We declare the right of the people of Ireland to the ownership of Ireland, and to the unfettered control of Irish destinies, to be sovereign and indefeasible. The long usurpation of that right by a foreign people and government has not extinguished the right, nor can it ever be extinguished except by the destruction of the Irish people. In every generation the Irish people have asserted their right to national freedom and sovereignty: six times during the past three hundred years they have asserted it in arms. Standing on that fundamental right and again asserting it in arms in the face of the world, we hereby proclaim the Irish Republic as a Sovereign Independent State, and we pledge our lives and the lives of our comrades-in-arms to the cause of its freedom, of its welfare, and its exaltation among the nations.

The Irish Republic is entitled to, and hereby claims, the allegiance of every Irishman and Irishwoman. The Republic guarantees religious and civil liberty, equal rights and equal opportunities to all its citizens, and declares its resolve to pursue the happiness and prosperity of the whole nation and of all its parts, cherishing all the children of the nation equally, and oblivious of the differences carefully fostered by an alien government, which have divided a minority from the majority in the past.

Until our arms have brought the opportune moment for the establishment of a permanent National Government, representative of the whole people of Ireland and elected by the suffrages of all her men and women, the Provisional Government, hereby constituted, will administer the civil and military affairs of the Republic in trust for the people.

We place the cause of the Irish Republic under the protection of the Most High God, Whose blessing we invoke upon our arms, and we pray that no one who serves that cause will dishonour it by cowardice, inhumanity, or rapine. In this supreme hour, the Irish nation must, by its valour and discipline and by the readiness of its children to sacrifice themselves for the common good, prove itself worthy of the august destiny to which it is called.

Signed on behalf of the Irish Republic to the People
THOMAS J CLARKE,
SEAN MacDIARMADA,
THOMAS MacDONAGH,
PH PEARSE,
EAMONN CEANNT,
JAMES CONNOLLY,
JOSEPH PLUNKETT

OLD PICTURE, NEW CAPTION

The new smoking ban wasn't always that easy to enforce.

Article of Ireland's Succession Act ensuring a spouse gets half of the 111 estate if the testator leaves no children

HANGING

Irishman Michael Barrett was the last person to be publicly hanged in Britain. On 26 May 1868 he was executed at Newgate in England for the Fenian bombing at Clerkenwell, which killed seven.

QUOTE UNQUOTE

Only Irish coffee provides in a single glass all four essential food groups: alcohol, caffeine, sugar, and fat.
Alex Levine, food writer

THE GROWTH OF DUBLIN

Dublin began as a landing place for Vikings in the ninth century and grew from a trading post to its present size, where the greater Dublin area spills over into adjoining counties.

Many of Dublin's city institutions were founded in the nineteenth century.

Dublin City Council was established under the 1840 Municipal Corporation Reform (Ireland) Act. This act widened the civic franchise to all householders with property of a rateable valuation worth more than £10 yearly. The city assembly was replaced by the more democratic city council.

In October 1841, Daniel O'Connell became the first Lord Mayor of Dublin.

Under the 1849 Dublin Improvement Act, the council assumed the duties of the Wide Streets Commission. In 1852 the council moved to the Royal Exchange, which was renamed City Hall.

From 1875 onwards, the council was given power to build housing for the working classes. After the passing of the Open Spaces Act, it began to acquire property for conversion into public parks.

Public libraries were opened at Thomas Street and Capel Street in 1884, and the city's first electricity power station was opened in Fleet Street in 1892. The council began motor registration in 1908, and the Dublin Main Drainage Scheme was also completed that year.

Dublin was the first city in either Ireland or Britain to allocate an official residence to its incumbent Lord Mayor. The mayor may reside in the official residence with his or her family.

In Ireland a protuberance like Primrose Hill, or, at most, Hindhead, looks like a mountain haunted by giants. You may be fresh from surmounting every pass in the Tyrol, but when you are faced by a trumpery lane through the Kerry mountains, you are filled with vague terrors: it seems dangerous to venture in and impossible to get out, even if you do not meet another car on a track that looks a tight fit for one. In Galway, south of the way, you find stone fields instead of grass ones, and in those fields cattle gravely crop the granite and seem to thrive on it. You travel on roads that are far more like the waves of the sea than the famous billowy pavement of St Mark's in Venice.

In the north there are no stone fields, but you come to a common green one with a little stagnant pool in the corner, and from that magic pool you are amazed to see a rush of waters through a narrow, deep, sinuous ditch, which ditch is the mighty Shannon emerging from the underworld. Rivers in Ireland duck like porpoises and then come to the surface and charge along it for a space and duck again. If you are afraid to penetrate a country so full of marvels, you can stay in a hotel in Dublin and yet be within half an hour's drive by car of moors as wild as you have often travelled many hundreds of miles from London to reach in the remotest parts of Scotland, and of coast scenery after which most English 'seaside resorts' will seem mere dust heaps on the banks of a dirty canal.

On the west coast you can struggle for an hour and a half up an endless succession of mountain brows, each of which looks like the top until you get there and see the next one towering above you; and when you are at last exhausted and filled with a conviction that you are enchanted and doomed to climb there forever, you suddenly recoil from a sheer drop of two thousand feet to the Atlantic, with nothing but salt water between you and America. You can watch affrightedly a bull's mouth of which the grinders are black, merciless rocks and the boiling spittle Atlantic rollers. You can make strange voyages to uncanny islands which carry to its highest the curious power of Ireland to disturb and excite the human imagination; and, if one of these voyages leads you in an open boat through seven or eight miles of ocean waves and tide races to Skellig Michael, it is not after the fashion of this world.

> **George Bernard Shaw,**
> **'Touring in Ireland' from**
> ***The Matter with Ireland*, 1962**

Number of houses in the seventeenth century village of Kill, near Dublin, 113
whose population was 100 people

QUOTE UNQUOTE

There are only two dialects of Irish, plain Irish and toothless Irish, and, lacking a proper acquaintance with the latter, I think I missed the cream of the old man's talk.
Frank O'Connor, Irish poet, playwright and biographer

DUBLIN PARKS

The brothers Benjamin Lee Guinness and Arthur (Lord Ardilaun) built up an estate in North Dublin and called it St Anne's after the holy well of the same name on the lands. Ardilaun had no children and the estate passed to their nephew Bishop Plunkett in the 1920s. He sold it in 1939 to the city council. In 1975, the famous St Anne's Rose Garden was opened to the public. Since 1981 it has been a centre for international rose trials.

PAPER TRAILS

The Nation was set up as a political paper in October 1842 by Charles Gavan Duffy, John Blake Dillon and Thomas Davis, who were all central figures in the group later known as Young Ireland. Its first day print-run of 12,000 copies sold out, and the paper quickly attracted strong writers of the time. The paper later ceased publication and the title is now used by Fianna Fáil, the governing party, for its party newsletter.

EUROVISION

Ireland hosted the Eurovision Song Contest in 1993 in Millstreet, Cork. Ireland also won the competition – with 'In Your Eyes' performed by Niamh Kavanagh.

Ireland had another winner in 1994 at the Eurovision Song Contest, which was again held in the Republic – this time in Dublin. Paul Harrington and Charlie McGettigan won with 'Rock 'n' Roll Kids'. The song was written by Brendan Graham, who was to bring Ireland even more success two years later.

Brendan Graham wrote the music and lyrics of 'The Voice', the song that won the Eurovision Song Contest in 1996 in Oslo, Norway. It was performed by Eimear Quinn.

Letter from David Lloyd George to Eamon de Valera, President of Ireland, dated 24 June 1921, in which he invites de Valera to attend a conference that will aim to resolve the Irish conflict.

Sir,

The British Government are deeply anxious that, so far as they can assure it, the King's appeal for reconciliation in Ireland shall not have been made in vain. Rather than allow yet another opportunity of settlement in Ireland to be cast aside, they felt it incumbent upon them to make a final appeal, in the spirit of the King's words, for a conference between themselves and the representatives of Southern and Northern Ireland, I write, therefore, to convey the following invitation to you as the chosen leader of the great majority in Southern Ireland, and to Sir James Craig, the Premier of Northern Ireland:

(1) That you should attend a conference here in London, in company with Sir James Craig, to explore to the utmost the possibility of a settlement.

(2) That you should bring with you for the purpose any colleagues whom you may select. The Government will, of course, give a safe conduct to all who may be chosen to participate in the conference.

We make this invitation with a fervent desire to end the ruinous conflict which has for centuries divided Ireland and embittered the relations of the peoples of these two islands, who ought to live in neighbourly harmony with each other, and whose co-operation would mean so much not only to the Empire but to humanity.

We wish that no endeavour should be lacking on our part to realise the King's prayer, and we ask you to meet us, as we will meet you, in the spirit of conciliation for which His Majesty appealed.

I am, Sir, your obedient servant,
D Lloyd George

Letter from Eamon de Valera, Mansion House, Dublin to David Lloyd George, dated 28 June 1921.

Sir,

I have received your letter. I am in consultation with such of the principal representatives of our nation as are available. We most earnestly desire to help in bringing about a lasting peace between the peoples of these two islands, but see no avenue by which it can be reached if you deny Ireland's essential unity and set aside the principle of national self-determination.

Before replying more fully to your letter, I am seeking a conference with certain representatives of the political minority in this country.

Eamon de Valera

LOVE ME DEARLY

A long-running affair between a married Irish Taoiseach and a married woman, which started in 1972, was an open secret in political circles in Dublin. Charles Haughey TD and society writer Terry Keane, who was married to a High Court judge, were lovers according to Keane, who revealed her decades-long affair on RTÉ television's live *The Late Late Show* in 1999. She returned in 2006 to the same show to say she regretted her first admission. Haughey died in 2006 following a long battle with cancer.

RECORD BREAKERS

The largest Irish dance involved 7,664 participants. It was organised by Cork City Council on 10 September 2005. The council had expected 11,500 people.

Seven dance zones were laid out along the South Mall and Grand Parade, and dancers had to dance for at least six minutes.

FAMOUS IRISHMEN: PERCY FRENCH

Songwriter Percy French is well-remembered for his popular ballads written in the nineteenth century. The Roscommon man toured Canada, the United States, the West Indies and England with his banjo, composing and singing comic songs.

In a *cause celébré*, French sued the directors of the West Clare Railway Company for loss of earnings when he and his troupe were late for a performance in Kilkee in 1898.

Arriving in Ennis from Dublin, they were on time for the 12.30 train, which was due to reach Kilkee at 3.30pm. However, the train failed en route and five hours elapsed before a replacement arrived.

French was too late for the show, and most of the audience had gone home when he arrived.

A company official explained that some weeds got into the boiler when the engine took on water on the way. Further down the track, the driver put out the fire because of the possibility of an explosion, and a replacement engine was requested.

French was awarded £10 compensation. The railway company appealed, but the award stood and a song lampooning the company, 'Are Ye Right There, Michael, Are You Right?', was born.

Don McClean recorded French's song 'Mountains of Mourne' in 1974.

In 2001, the Minister for Finance introduced a new savings scheme called Special Savings Incentive Accounts (SSIA). For every amount saved, the Exchequer contributed an additional 25% to the individual saver's account. Savers agreed to put money aside each month. To benefit fully from the scheme, they had to leave savings in the account for five years.

The maximum that could be saved per month was set at €254.

A 2006 survey detailed how it was expected that matured SSIA funds would be spent:

- Consumer items *31.2%*
- Savings, pensions and investments *46.1%*
- Debt repayment *10.3%*
- Other items *12.4%*

RELIGIOUS EVENTS

A papal mass celebrated by Pope John Paul II in 1979 saw a million and a quarter people – almost one in every three citizens – arrive in Phoenix Park on the same day to greet the only pope ever to visit Ireland.

THE OGAM ALPHABET

Ogam is the earliest form of writing in Ireland and was used between the bronze and early Christian periods.

The Ogam alphabet is made up of a series of up to five strokes along or across a line. It was designed specifically for the Irish language and was originally put to use in order to commemorate named persons. Letters written in Ogam were carved on standing stones using the edge of the stone as the centre line.

The writing consists of sets of strokes diagonally through, horizontally through or just to one side of an imaginary axis.

Ogam normally reads from the left-hand side bottom up, across the top and down the right-hand side. Half of the letters of the alphabet take their names from trees. The oldest Ogam inscriptions known were written on stone. These date from about the fifth century to about the seventh century. From then on the Ogam language was mainly used by students of poetry and grammar. This later form was written on manuscripts – ensuring its survival into modern times.

Number of countries visited by Pope John Paul II, including Ireland 117 (in 1979) which was third, after Poland and Mexico

*Davey was confident he'd finally found a way
to cross the bogs safely.*

IRISH RIDDLE

What was the name for Ireland in Julius Caesar's time?
Answer on page 153.

THINGS TO SEE IN OFFALY

Between 1845 and the early 1900s, the telescope at Birr Castle in
Co Offaly was the largest in the world. It was built in Ireland by Irish
engineers for William Parsons, the third Earl of Rosse. The telescope
was dismantled in 1914, but it was later restored as a testament to
the achievements of the past.

Ireland's state broadcasting began in January 1926 and emanated from a single room studio on Denmark Street in Dublin. Patriotic ballads, poems and stories were the order of the day. There had recently been a civil war (1922-1923), and listeners to the new national station were drawn from both sides of the divide.

Little talk radio was broadcast lest offence be caused to one group or the other, and it was believed that common ground could be found in Ireland's cultural heritage.

The station was named 2RN by the British Post Office, the authority responsible for it at the time, and it is thought that this moniker was inspired by the last three syllables of the song 'Come Back To Erin'. 2RN was broadcast with a 1.5kW Marconi Q-type transmitter, which was housed in a hut in McKee Barracks on the high ground beside Phoenix Park.

The service expanded in 1927 when a 1kW sister station, 6CK, opened in Cork. It was located in a former women's jail, which now houses the Radio Museum Experience. 6CK remained on air until 1930.

From 7.30pm each evening, listeners were given a tuning note, generally a steady tone, to enable them to tune in their valve receiver or crystal set to receive broadcasts, all of which were live. Tape recording was introduced at the end of 1949, allowing for re-use, longer recording and easier editing, but reception could be difficult or erratic, especially at a distance of more than 32 kilometres away from Dublin or Cork.

Radio sets did not have the built-in aerials that they do today. It was necessary to connect the crystal or valve wireless set to a long wire aerial and an earth to hear broadcasts.

In 1928, 2RN moved from its single studio in Denmark Street into new headquarters in the General Post Office (GPO), which had been reconstructed after shelling by British forces during the 1916 Rising. The station now had three studios – one for drama, one for music and one for the announcer. Heady times.

2RN covered the World Eucharistic Congress in Dublin in 1932, using a new high-powered 60kW transmitter installed at Athlone in the middle of the country.

The event was relayed by the BBC and several national stations in continental Europe.

Sponsored programmes were introduced as a method of advertising in the early days, and advertising revenue became increasingly important to cover the station's costs.

The radio station moved location to Donnybrook in 1961, when *Telefís Éireann* began broadcasting, and today all stations operate under the corporate RTÉ banner.

When I said good-bye to Donegal I went into Northern Ireland. An English reader who has not studied the map will wonder how I performed such an unnatural feat. It is simple.

Donegal, the most northerly county in Ireland and topographically in Ulster, is not in Northern Ireland! It is Free State territory. When the Irish Free State was established six of the nine counties of Ulster expressed themselves ready to die rather than become a part of it. They decided to form themselves into a political entity with a parliament of their own. And this is Northern Ireland.

The six counties that compose it are Fermanagh, Tyrone, Londonderry, Antrim, Down, and Armagh. The three Ulster counties under the Free State flag are Donegal, Caven, and Monaghan. The last two, forming, as they do, the southern boundary of Ulster, melt naturally into the Free State, but Donegal in the north is cut off in the most untidy and inconvenient manner from her parent. She looks almost like an orphan or a foundling. There is a little back door to her on the south about five miles wide (from Bundoran to Belleek) but the rest of her eastern boundary is on the frontier.

It thus happens that when you are in Donegal you can look south into Northern Ireland, and when you are in either in Londonderry, Tyrone, or Fermangh you can look north into Southern Ireland! This is no doubt an excellent joke except to those who have to live in it! It must be exasperating to find yourself barred by a customs barrier from the country town in which you have always enjoyed free trading.

But as long as it profits the Free State to build up her enterprises behind a tariff wall, or as long as Northern Ireland remains outside the Free State (which, I am told, will be for ever), this inconvenient and costly boundary with its double line of officials will remain, the only frontier in the British Isles.

HV Morton, *In Search of Ireland*, 1930

AMERICAN IRISH

Mike Quill, a native of Co Kerry, founded the Transport Workers Union of America in 1934, and was its first international president.

Quill took part in the 1916 Irish rebellion. Afterwards he left for the United States. He is most remembered for his role in the 1966 transit strike in New York City. When an injunction was issued to halt the strike, Quill tore up the injunction in front of television cameras, after which he was jailed.

120 *Height in metres of the Spire on Dublin's O'Connell Street, unveiled in 2003*

QUOTE UNQUOTE

*Ah, Ireland... That damnable, delightful country, where everything
that is right is the opposite of what it ought to be.*
Benjamin Disraeli, UK prime minister

NEVER SHORT OF A WELL-TURNED PHRASE:
SIX IRISH SAYINGS

A light heart lives longest
Maireann croí éadrom i bhfad

A (true) friend's eye is a good mirror
Is maith an scáthán súil charad

A beetle recognises another beetle
Aithníonn ciaróg ciaróg eile

Many a time a man's mouth broke his nose
Is minic a bhris béal duine a shrón

Hunger is a tasty sauce
Is maith an t-anlann an t-ocras

Never take advice without a woman's guidance
Ná glac pioc comhairle gan comhairle ban

THE ORIGINS OF HALLOWE'EN

Hallowe'en was originally a Celtic festival that celebrated the advent
of winter. On 1 November, Celts used to celebrate Samhain as the
doorway between light and dark, the two seasons in the Celtic year.
The most important part of the festival was night, because the Celts
believed that this was where the day began.

Following the arrival of Christianity, Samhain was changed to All
Saints' Day, or Hallowmass, and the night before became Hallowe'en.
The second day of November became All Souls' Day, during which
people can offer prayers for those lost in the year.

Samhain represented the ascendancy of the dark – when farmers
would bring their livestock down from the hill pastures, and harvests
were gathered to prevent the fairies from blowing away the remaining
produce in November.

*Number of expatriate staff employed by Irish NGO GOAL on 121
humanitarian programmes in 20 countries in 2003*

ORDERS

The Orange Order is the largest Protestant organisation in Northern Ireland. It also has lodges in the Republic of Ireland. In 1795, a clash between Protestants and Catholics led some of those involved to swear an oath to uphold the Protestant faith and be loyal to King William III and his heirs, giving birth to the Orange Order.

PERSONAL MATTERS

An annual Global Sex Survey carried out online in Ireland by Durex came up with the following results in 2005:

Average age when first received sex education: **13.1 years**
Average age of first sex: **17.3 years**
Average number of sexual partners: **11.1**
Unprotected sex: **58%**
Unplanned pregnancy, under 16 years of age: **2%**
Unplanned pregnancy, 17-18 years of age: **4%**
Unplanned pregnancy, aged more than 19: **9%**
Sexually transmitted disease (STI): **5%**
No pregnancy and no STI: **85%**

IRISH INVENTORS

A man who designed and built a new plough was also the first Irishman to fly.

Harry Ferguson was nicknamed the mad mechanic, more in admiration than malice. He designed and built a new plough that coupled to a tractor in three-point linkage to form a single unit. His Ferguson System, patented in 1926, changed methods of farming for the better.

Ferguson also designed and built his own motorcycle, racing car and a monoplane, which he flew on New Year's Eve 1909 at Hillsborough, Co Down, thus making the first powered flight in Ireland. The plane travelled a total distance of 118.5 metres.

From 1911 onwards, Ferguson sold tractors to Irish farmers more accustomed to horse-drawn ploughs than machines with engines.

By 1926, the principal patent of the Ferguson System was granted. In 1938, Ferguson and Henry Ford reached an agreement by which Ford's American company could manufacture tractors to Ferguson's designs. He died in 1960.

Along Dublin bay, on a sunny July morning, the public gardens along the Dalkey tramline look bright as a series of parasols. Chalk-blue sea appears at the ends of the roads of villas turning downhill – but these are still the suburbs, not the seaside. In the distance, floating across the bay, buildings glitter out of the heat-haze on the neck to Howth, and Howth Head looks higher veiled. After inland Ballsbride, the tram from Dublin speeds up; it zooms through the residential reaches with the gathering steadiness of a launched ship. Its red velvet seating accommodation is seldom crowded – its rival, the quicker bus, lurches ahead of it down the same road.

After Ballsbridge, the ozone smell of the bay sifts more and more through the smell of the chimneys and pollen and the July darkened garden trees as the bay and line converge. Then at a point you see the whole bay open – there are nothing but flats of grass and the sunk railway between the running tram and the still sea. An immense glaring reflection floods through the tram. When high terraces, backs to the tramline, shut out of view again, even their backs have a salted, marine air; their cotton window-blinds are pulled half down, crooked; here and there an inner door left open let you see a flash of sea through a house.

The weathered lions on gate posts ought to be dolphins. Red low lying villas have been fitted between earlier terraces, ornate, shabby, glassy hotels, bow fronted mansions all built in the first place to stand up over spaces of grass. Looks from trams and voices from public gardens invade the old walled lawns with their grottos and weeping willows. Spit-and-polish alternatives with decay. But stucco, slate and slate-fronts, blotched Italian pink-wash, dusty windows, lace curtains and dolphin-lions seem to be the eternity of this tram route. Quite soon the modern will sag, chip, fade. Change leaves everything at the same level. Nothing stays bright but mornings.

Elizabeth Bowen,
'Unwelcome Idea' from
Collected Stories

PAPER TRAILS

The *United Irishman* was first published in Dublin in March 1899 and was edited by Sinn Féin's founder, Arthur Griffith, a printer by trade. In 1906, the *United Irishman* collapsed under a libel suit. An earlier nineteenth-century *United Irishman* was founded by John Mitchel after he left *The Nation*, but it, too, ceased publication.

Number of passengers who embarked on the fateful voyage of the Titanic 123 from Cobh in Co Cork on 11 April 1912

THE TOUR DE FRANCE

In 1963 Shay Elliott became the first Irishman to wear the leader's yellow jersey in the Tour de France. It was won that year by Jacques Anquetil of France.

In 1987 Stephen Roche became the first Irishman to win the Tour de France. In that year he also won the World Championship, and the Tour of Italy.

The Tour de France raced through Ireland in 1998 as part of its outlying stages. That year's event was marred by revelations of drug-taking by some of the cyclists. It was won eventually by Marco Pantani of Italy.

A SONG FOR IRELAND

Paul McCartney and Wings had a hit in 1972 with Paul's song 'Give Ireland Back to the Irish'. While it was a well-meant song, few in Westminster came out in support of its sentiments, and it was banned from being played on air by the BBC.

FORGOTTEN ISLANDS

The Blasket Islands, situated off the southwest coast of the Dingle peninsula, Co Kerry, were once home to a thriving population. The main island, Great Blasket, was abandoned in 1953 and remains uninhabited to this day.

The islanders were a friendly bunch and made links with Spanish, English and French fisherman. Indeed, Pierre Trehiou, a French fisherman, traded rum, tobacco and other items with the islanders in lieu of their lobster catch. Trehiou would haul the lobsters back to the continent alive in a net on the bottom of his ship.

However, the population began to decline in 1917, and only two couples were married on the island between then and the 1953 exodus. By then, there were just 22 inhabitants.

'Blasket Writers' is a term that refers to authors from Irish-speaking Catholic communities living near the islands on the west coast. The group includes Maurice O'Sullivan (1904-1950), Peig Sayers (1873-1958) and Tomás Ó Criomhthain (1856-1937), who wrote *An tOileánach* (*The Islandman*), which records the islanders' traditions and way of life.

A lament in one ear, maybe,
but always a song in the other.
Sean O'Casey, Irish dramatist and memoirist

LIP-SMACKING FARE:
SOME FAMOUS IRISH DISHES

Beef and Irish stout
A simple and satisfying stew

Colcannon
A concoction of potato and cabbage

Champ
Similar to colcannon, but with added spring onions, milk and butter

Soda bread
A moreish loaf made with buttermilk

Barm brack
Tasty fruit bread

Crubeens
Pig's trotters, cooked with carrots and onions or fried in breadcrumbs

Bacon and cabbage
Boiled together for a tasty main course

Boxty pancakes with black pudding, bacon and mustard cream
Griddled potato cakes, plus trimmings

Potato bread
A prime gap-filler that sits in the stomach

GONE BUT NOT FORGOTTEN

The Millennium Clock was nicknamed 'Chime in the Slime'. The clock was placed beneath the surface of Dublin's River Liffey and supposed to count down to the new millennium. However, there were technical problems, including the formation of a film over the clock's face, which obscured the numerals. The clock was removed in 1999.

Number of authors related to County Waterford that have samples of 125
their work published together in The Writers of County Waterford

IRISH INVENTIONS

Belfast's Samuel Davidson was accredited with many inventions, including tea-drying equipment, the forward-bladed centrifugal fan and even a hand-held howitzer.

He was clearly a man of whom to take notice, and was in fact knighted. Indeed, in a salute to local inventors, the Northern Bank issued a £50 note featuring Davidson.

THE FEAST OF THE DEAD

If 1 November is the first day of winter, Hallowe'en (31 October) is the welcoming party – a night of feasting, merrymaking and divination. The Catholic church designated the first day of November as All Saints' or All Hallows Day. So, All Hallows Eve became Hallowe'en. But for the Celts, Hallowe'en was also celebrated as the Feast of the Dead, a time when the dead were said to revisit the mortal world.

It is also a night of spirits. According to Irish legend, a malicious fairy, known as the *púca*, is wont to spit on wild fruit on Hallowe'en so that nobody can dine on berries as winter progresses. Many families leave unused produce out on the night to feed the fairy host as it proceeds to blast all berries, thistles, ragworth and hedgerows with its breath.

Traditional Irish Hallowe'en foods include colcannon – boiled potato, curly kale cabbage and raw onions. Coins are wrapped in baking paper and placed in dinners for children to find. Hallowe'en barm brack, a fruit bread with things hidden in it, is sliced and given to each person. If you find a rag, it suggests your financial future is doubtful. A coin, however, presages a prosperous year. A ring is a sign of romance, continued happiness or marriage.

Nowadays, as in many other places in the world, young children dress in scary costumes and go house to house for a 'Trick or Treat', while the older children light bonfires, often unaware they are continuing a centuries-old tradition.

In ancient times, to celebrate the start of winter, druids built huge sacred bonfires, and people brought produce and sacrificed animals to share at a communal dinner in celebration.

After the festival, people re-lit household fires from the sacred bonfire to help protect and keep them warm during winter.

Nowadays, householders drag garden cuttings and unwanted domestic furniture to the fire and set them ablaze. They may also seek spirits in bottles – and some may even bring them home!

*Many visitors found the Irish road
signs very confusing.*

A LIBRARY FOR THE NATION

Knighted by the Queen Elizabeth II in 1954, New Yorker Chester
Beatty became the first honorary citizen of Ireland three years later.
He founded the Chester Beatty Library to store his collection of
Arabic manuscripts, and Chinese and Japanese works of art. He
bequeathed the library to the people of Ireland on his death in 1968.

Distance in kilometres between Dublin in the east of Leinster and 127
Athlone on the western rim of the province

Which president of Israel was born in Ireland?
Answer on page 153.

IRISH OBSERVATIONS

The Irish have been always remarkable for their funeral lamentations; and this peculiarity has been noticed by almost every traveller who visited them; and it seems derived from their Celtic ancestors, the primaeval inhabitants of this isle...

It has been affirmed of the Irish, that to cry was more natural to them than to any other nation, and at length the Irish cry became proverbial...

[...]

It is curious to observe how customs and ceremonies degenerate. The present Irish cry, or howl, cannot boast of such melody, nor is the funeral procession conducted with much dignity. The crowd of people who assemble at these funerals sometimes amounts to a thousand, often to four or five hundred. They gather as the bearers of the hearse proceed on their way, and when they pass through any village, or when they come near any houses, they begin to cry – Oh! Oh! Oh! Oh! Oh! Agh! Agh! raising their notes from the first OH! to the last AGH! in a kind of mournful howl. This gives notice to the inhabitants of the village that a FUNERAL IS PASSING and immediately they flock out to follow it. In the province of Munster it is a common thing for the women to follow a funeral, to join in the universal cry with all their might and main for some time, and then to turn and ask – 'Arrah! who is it that's dead? – who is it we're crying for?'

Even the poorest people have their own burying-places – that is, spots of ground in the churchyards where they say that their ancestors have been buried ever since the wars of Ireland; and if these burial-places are ten miles from the place where a man dies, his friends and neighbours take care to carry his corpse thither. Always one priest, often five or six priests, attend these funerals; each priest repeats a mass, for which he is paid, sometimes a shilling, sometimes half a crown, sometimes half a guinea, or a guinea, according to their circumstances, or, as they say, according to the ability of the deceased. After the burial of any very poor man, who has left a widow or children, the priest makes what is called a COLLECTION for the widow; he goes round to every person present, and each contributes sixpence or a shilling, or what they please. The reader will find, in the note upon the word WAKE, more particulars respecting the conclusion of the Irish funerals.

Maria Edgeworth,
Castle Rackrent, 1800

TOMBS

Newgrange passage tomb is Ireland's best known prehistoric monument. Dating from about 3,200BC, the Co Meath tomb is many centuries older than both Stonehenge and the great pyramids of Egypt.

It is part of a complex in the Boyne Valley that includes the monuments at Knowth and Dowth.

EXCHEQUER FUNDING OF QUALIFIED POLITICAL PARTIES IN 2005

Fianna Fáil (79 seats) – €4,597,103

Fine Gael (32 seats) – €3,137,147

Labour Party (21 seats) – €1,942,564

Progressive Democrats (eight seats) – €907,479

Green Party (six seats) – €670,337

Sinn Féin (five seats) – €606,002

Socialist Party (one seat) – €58,759

Total €11,919,391

Some 14 independent TDs did not qualify
for funding under this heading.

RECORD BREAKERS

Strokestown Park, an eighteenth-century Palladian mansion and estate in Co Roscommon, has the longest herbaceous border in Ireland or Britain. The estate's stables also house a large private archive on the Great Famine.

The world's largest permanent hedge maze is the Peace Maze at Castlewellan Forest Park, Co Down, Northern Ireland. It has a total area of 1.1 hectares and a path length of 3.5 kilometres.

The tallest box hedge in Ireland is 11 metres high and grows at Birr Castle, Co Offaly. It is at least three centuries old. Birr Castle was also the home of the Great Telescope, which was the largest telescope in the world for more than 70 years.

IRISH RIDDLE

Where was the world's first commuter line opened?
Answer on page 153.

IRISH INVENTIONS

Mayo-born Louis Brennan invented the world's first guided missile –
a torpedo used as an early coastal defence mechanism. Brennan also
designed a monorail and helicopter. He was engaged by the British
Air Ministry in aircraft research. A large sum was spent on the
invention of a helicopter, but in 1926 the Air Ministry gave up
working on it – which only goes to show how much they knew!

QUITE A MAN

When the classic film *The Quiet Man*, directed by John Ford, was
released on video, it sold 200,000 copies in Britain alone within
four years.

Although many Irish people discount the 1951 film as a large dose of
paddywhackery, in 1996 it was voted the most popular Irish film of all
time by readers of *The Irish Times*.

It is based on a short story written by Maurice Walsh, a Kerryman who
lived and worked in Scotland as a customs officer before returning to
Dublin on transfer in 1922. He is buried in Lucan, Co Dublin.

Meanwhile, on the west coast, in Cong, Co Mayo, where the film was
shot, a *Quiet Man* industry has grown up to cater for tourists.

The film starred John Wayne, Maureen O'Hara, Victor McLaglen and
Barry Fitzgerald, an actor who cut his teeth at The Abbey Theatre, the
National Theatre of Ireland.

Sean Thornton (John Wayne) returns from the United States to reclaim
his homestead and escape his past. His eye is caught by Mary Kate
Danaher (Maureen O'Hara), younger sister of the ill-tempered 'Red'
Will Danaher (Victor McLaglen). The relationship between Sean and
Mary Kate, punctuated by Will's wild attempts to separate them, forms
the plot, with Sean's past as a boxer involved in a fatal match provides
a gripping back story. Fitzgerald hammed it up for all he was worth as
a local character.

Down in the North the loyalty is intense and loud. An opinion favourable to the principles of the Land League it would be hardly prudent to express. Any dissatisfaction with anything at all is seldom expressed for fear of being classed with these troublers of Ireland.

The weather is very inclement, and has been ever since I landed. Snow, rain, hail, sleet, hard frost, mud, have alternated. Some days have been one continuous storm of either snow or sleet.

The roads through Antrim are beautifully clean and neat, not only on the line of rail but along the country roads inland. The land is surely beautiful, exceedingly, and kept like a garden. The number of houses of some, nay of great, pretensions, is most astonishing. Houses set in spacious and well-kept grounds, with porter lodges, terraced lawns, conservatories, &c., abound. They succeed one another so constantly that one wonders how the land is able to bear them all, or by what means such universal grandeur is supported. There is an outcry of want, of very terrible hard times, but certainly the country shows no signs thereof. The great wonder to me is where the labourers who produce all this neatness and beauty live? Where are the small farmers on whom the high rent presses so heavily? Few houses, where such could by any possibility be housed, are to be seen from the roadside. There are so very few cottages and so very many gentlemen's houses that I am forced to believe that the peasantry have almost entirely disappeared. Yet I know there must be labourers somewhere to keep the place so beautiful.

Margaret Moran Dixon McDougall, *The Letters of 'Norah' on Her Tour Through Ireland, Being a Series of Letters to the Montreal 'Witness' as Special Correspondent to Ireland*

QUOTE UNQUOTE

There is no language like the Irish for soothing and quieting.
John Millington Synge, dramatist, poet and writer

AMERICAN IRISH

James Hoban from Co Kilkenny was the architect who designed the White House. He won the competition for the design of a mansion for the President (later called the White House), which he built from 1792 to 1799 and rebuilt after it was destroyed by the British in 1814.

Number of houses on a single street that constituted Wicklow's Carnew 131 *town in Samuel Lewis' 1837 Topographical Dictionary of Ireland*

Lovers all over the world celebrate on 14 February with a nod towards St Valentine, the patron saint of lovers – but few know the good saint's bones are lying in Dublin.

In 1835, John Spratt, an Irish Carmelite preacher, visited Rome where his style attracted praise and where many were moved to present him with gifts of appreciation. One such gift was from Pope Gregory XVI. To Spratt's surprise, it proved to be the remains of St Valentine. Not wishing to look a gift-giving pope in the mouth, Spratt brought his new possession home as a souvenir.

The reliquary containing the remains arrived in Dublin on 10 November 1836. It was brought in solemn procession to Whitefriar Street Church to be received by Archbishop Murray of Dublin.

However, once the procession and media opportunity were over and the preacher had died, interest in things associated with him declined and the relics were placed in storage.

There was renewed interest in the saint in the 1960s, and an altar and shrine were constructed to house the relics and enable them to be venerated. But there were several saints of the same name, all of whom died as martyrs. One Valentine was a Roman priest martyred under the Emperor Claudius II in 270AD; another was a bishop of Terni who was killed in the same century.

The Dublin friars hold a letter of authenticity, from Pope Gregory XVI, which accompanied the remains to Dublin.

There are Italian claims that some remains found in the Church of St Praxedes in Rome are those of Valentine – though *which* Valentine this might be is not altogether clear.

Furthermore, friars at the church of Blessed St John Duns Scotus in Glasgow's Gorbals have held a special Valentine's service in February since 1999, putting on display what they claim are the martyr's bones. These relics are said to have been in the possession of a wealthy French Catholic family who arranged a permanent sanctuary for them in Glasgow in 1882.

The church belongs to the Irish Carmelites, who say the shrine is visited throughout the year by couples who come to pray to Valentine and ask him to watch over them in their lives together.

On 14 February, the feast day of the saint, many couples attend eucharistic celebrations in the church. The ceremonies include a Blessing of Rings for those about to marry.

The reliquary is removed from beneath the side altar and placed before the high altar in the church where it is venerated at the masses of the day. At the 11am and 3.15pm masses there are special sermons and also a short ceremony for the Blessing of Rings. Otherwise, the casket sits beneath the marble altar in a niche protected by an ornate iron and glass gate.

Above the altar stands the life-sized statue of the saint set into a marble mosaic alcove. The reliquary contains some of the remains of Saint Valentine – it is not claimed by the church that all of his remains are found in this casket.

Like love itself, the authenticity of Valentine's relics may be looked upon as a mystery to be enjoyed without too much soul-searching.

OLD PICTURE, NEW CAPTION

After a few drinks, the locals were never averse to breaking out into a chorus of 'Oh Danny Boy'.

RELIGIOUS EVENTS

The 31st Eucharistic Congress, held on 23 June 1932 in Phoenix Park, saw almost half a million people gather to witness papal legate Cardinal Lorenzo Lauri celebrate mass.

Contemporary accounts record the presence of church dignitaries, including nine cardinals, hundreds of bishops and other clerics, representing 48 countries.

INTERNATIONAL IRELAND

EI or EJ – Ireland's international civil aircraft markings
IRL – Ireland's international car registration
+353 – Ireland's international direct dial code
.ie – Ireland's official country-code domain name

BRIGHT SPARKS

In his quest for knowledge, the inventor of the induction coil used to practice electrocution on divinity students in Maynooth College.

Dundalk-born Nicholas Callan entered St Patrick's College, Maynooth, Co Kildare, in 1816 to study for the priesthood. While there, he became interested in electricity and magnetism. After ordination and his appointment to the chair of natural physics, he set up a laboratory in the basement of Maynooth College.

There were no instruments available to measure the strength of the current or the voltage – so Callan used the students as guinea pigs. One was hospitalised after receiving several doses of electricity; another was knocked unconscious by a single jolt. After Callan was banned from using students, he resorted to using chickens instead – who at least had no next-of-kin to complain on their behalf.

In 1836, Callan took a horseshoe-shaped iron bar and discovered that when he interrupted the current sent through the primary coil, a high voltage current was generated in the secondary coil. The faster he interrupted the current, the bigger the spark. He had discovered how a transformer works, going from low voltage in the first coil to high voltage in the second coil.

Callan spent the rest of his life in Maynooth experimenting with matters electrical and died in 1864.

An Irish cabin, in general, is like a little antediluvian ark; for husband, wife and children, cow and calf, pigs, poultry, dog, and frequently cat, repose under the same roof in perfect amity. A whimsical calculation sometime since ascertained that in eighty-seven cabins there were one hundred and twenty full grown pigs, and forty-seven dogs. The rent of cabin and potato plot in the county of Wicklow and neighbourhood, is from one to two guineas; the family live upon potatoes and butter-milk six days in the week, and instead of 'an added pudding', the Sabbath is generally celebrated by bacon and greens... The price of labour was sixpence halfpenny per day.

Insufficiency of provision, which operates so powerfully against marriage in England, is not known or cared about in Ireland; there the want of an establishment never affects the brain of the enamoured rustic. Love lingers only until he can find out a dry bank, pick a few sticks, collect some furze and fern, knead a little mud with straw, and raise a hut about six feet high, with a door to let in the light and let out the smoke; these accomplished, the happy pair, united by their priest, enter their sylvan dwelling, and a rapid race of chubby boys and girls soon proves by what scanty means life can be sustained and imparted.

Upon an average, a man, his wife, and four children, will eat thirty-seven pounds of potatoes a day. A whimsical anecdote is related of an Irish potato. An Englishman, seeing a number of fine florid children in a cabin, said to the father: 'How do your countrymen contrive to have so many fine children?' 'By Jasus it is the potato, Sir,' said he.

Three pounds of good mealy potatoes are more than equivalent to one pound of bread. It is worthy of remark to those who live well, without reflecting upon the condition of others to whom Providence has been less bountiful, that one individual who subsists upon meat and bread, consumes what would maintain five persons who live on bread alone, and twelve who subsist on potatoes.

John Carr,
A Stranger in Ireland, 1806

AN IRISH FIRST

Pat Falvey from Cork was the first Irishman to climb all the great mountains of the world, including Mount Everest, Kilimanjaro, Mount Vinson and Mount Aconcagua. He climbed the seven greatest summits between 1994 and 1997.

Distance in kilometres between the Viking settlements of Dublin 135 and Wexford

RECORD BREAKERS

Vincent Pilkington of Cootehill, Co Cavan, plucked a turkey in one minute and 30 seconds on 17 November 1980, to enter the *Guinness Book of Records*. The plucker later carried out 24 hours of turkey plucking to raise funds for his local Holy Family School. On that occasion, he is said to have plucked 244 turkeys in one day.

WISE WORDS

Irish proverbs from the older generation...

A drink precedes a story.

Time is a great storyteller.

Put silk on a goat, and it's still a goat.

It takes time to build castles. Rome was not built in a day.

The man with the boots does not mind where he places his foot.

If you do not sow in the spring, you will not reap in the autumn.

When the liquor was gone, the fun was gone.

There is no fireside like your own fireside.

It is not a secret if it is known by three people.

Good as drink is, it ends in thirst.

It is a long road that has no turning.

KNOCK SHRINE

Fifteen locals received the shock of their lives when Our Lady, the Virgin Mary, St Joseph and St John the Evangelist appeared at the south gable of the Church of St John the Baptist, Knock, Co Mayo, on 21 August 1879. Legend has it that they witnessed the apparition for two hours, in the pouring rain, though the gable itself remained perfectly dry.

Since then, Knock has become a shrine, with pilgrims flocking there to pray to Our Lady of Knock. In 1979, Pope John Paul II made the pilgrimage to the holy site to honour its centenary year. Mother Teresa visited in 1993, and it is estimated that around one and a half million pilgrims make the trip there every year.

136 *Section of the Irish Road Traffic Act that regulates annual inspection of taximeters*

FAIRY TALES

The fairy people, the *daione sidhe* (pronounced 'shee'), have been reported in Ireland since ancient times. Some say their name derives from *aes sidhe* (folk of the 'sidhe', or mound) from the large hillocks they are said to inhabit.

Two types of fairy are said to exist: the sociable 'trooping fairy' and the more introverted 'solitary fairy'. Trooping fairies are to be found in merry bands around Ireland's hawthorn bushes and sacred stone circles – the fairy 'raths'. These fairy raths crop up in pastures all over Ireland. Until recent times, they were always left unfarmed for fear of disturbing the fairies who live there, which was said to bring bad luck.

Ireland's most famous fairy is the leprechaun. Generally depicted as a small, old man (around 60 centimetres tall) with the cocked hat and leather apron of a shoemaker, the leprechaun is said to be aloof and unfriendly, preferring to live alone, making shoes and, of course, protecting his infamous pot of gold. If you capture a leprechaun, you can force him to reveal the whereabouts of his treasure – but, beware, for he is notoriously wily.

Ireland's most famous female fairy is the *bean-sidhe*, or banshee, the fairy woman whose loud wails are said to announce a death. Depicted as a white figure with long silver-grey hair, she is also known as the Lady of Sorrow or the Lady of Death.

QUOTE UNQUOTE

I come from the scraggy farm and moss,
Old patchworks that the pitch and toss
Of history has left disheveled.
Seamus Heaney, Irish poet

PAPER TRAILS

An Phoblacht/Republican News is Ireland's biggest-selling political weekly newspaper. With offices in Dublin and Belfast, it offers Sinn Féin analysis of all aspects of Irish politics. The newspaper incorporates the titles of two republican papers, *An Phoblacht* and *Republican News*, which amalgamated in January 1979.

Section of the Irish Defence Act that says you may not desert if you are 137
in the Defence Forces

AMERICAN IRISH

Commodore John Barry from Wexford is said to be the father of the US Navy. In his 58 years, he rose from a cabin boy to the senior commander of the entire fleet.

He was the first to capture a British war vessel on the high seas. He quelled three mutinies and captured more than 20 ships. He also authored a *Signal Book*, which established a set of signals used for effective communication between ships.

QUOTE UNQUOTE

Those who drink to forget, please pay in advance.
Sign at the Hibernian Bar, Cork City

IRISH OBSERVATIONS

It looks like the beginning of the world, somehow: the sea looks older than in other places, the hills and rocks strange, and formed differently from other rocks and hills-as those vast dubious monsters were formed who possessed the earth before man. The hill-tops are shattered into a thousand cragged fantastical shapes; the water comes swelling into scores of little strange creeks, or goes off with a leap, roaring into those mysterious caves yonder, which penetrate who knows how far into our common world?

The savage rock-sides are painted of a hundred colours. Does the sun ever shine here? Was the world was moulded and fashioned out of formless chaos this must have been the bit over – a remnant of chaos? Think of that! – it is a tailor's simile. Well, I am a Cockney: I wish I were in Pall Mall! Yonder is a kelp-burner: a lurid smoke from his burning kelp rises up to the leaden sky, and he looks as naked and fierce as Cain. Bubbling up out of the rocks at the very brim of the sea rises a little crystal spring: how comes it there? And there is an old grey hag beside, who has been there for hundreds and hundreds of years and there sits and sells whiskey at the extremity of creation! How do you dare to sell whiskey there, old woman? Did you serve old Saturn with a glass when he lay along the Causeway here? In reply she says, she has no change for a shilling: she never has; but her whiskey is good.

William Makepeace Thackeray, from *An Irish Sketchbook*, 1845

OLD PICTURE, NEW CAPTION

*Patrick and Seamus were the most eligible
bachelors in the village.*

A SONG FOR IRELAND

Irish country singer Gloria had a hit in the 1970s with her song
'One Day at a Time'. It was number one for 90 weeks.

TAXING IRELAND

Income tax is levied by the state on all income arising from
individuals, partnerships, and unincorporated bodies.

The lower tax rate is 20% up to €29,400 per annum, and the higher
rate is 42% on subsequent amounts, after any tax allowances have
been taken into consideration.

*Amount in millions of euro that were waged in on-course betting in 2004 139
at Irish greyhound tracks*

BOTTOMS UP

Some of Ireland's most colourful drinking toasts...

May you live as long as you want,
and never want as long as you live.

May you live to be 100 years, with one extra year to repent.

As you slide down the banisters of life may the splinters never point
the wrong way.

May your neighbours respect you, trouble neglect you, the angels
protect you, and heaven accept you.

May your pockets be heavy and your heart be light, may good luck
pursue you each morning and night.

May I see you grey and combing your children's hair.

May you die in bed at 95 years, shot by a jealous
husband (or wife).

May you have the hindsight to know where you've been, the
foresight to know where you're going and the insight to know when
you've gone too far.

May the frost never afflict your spuds, may the outside leaves of
your cabbage always be free from worms, may the crow never pick
your haystack – and may your donkey always be in foal.

IRISH RIDDLE

When was a world land speed record set in Ireland?
Answer on page 153.

AN IRISH CHRISTMAS

Christmas may come only once a year, but in Ireland it lasts, more or
less, for a whole month. It opens on 8 December, the Feast of the
Immaculate Conception (and the start of Christmas shopping in many
of Ireland's urban centres), and doesn't properly wind up until
6 January, the Feast of the Epiphany.

THE DEATH PENALTY

The last ever hanging in Ireland took place in 1954, with the last public hanging held in 1865. The punishment was removed from the Irish penal code in 1990, but was only completely removed from the Irish constitution after a referendum on 7 June 2001.

Some 62% of voters were in favour of removing capital punishment from the Constitution, and so the 21st Amendment was added, which prevents the Irish Houses of Parliament, or *Oireachtas*, from enacting 'any law providing for the imposition of the death penalty'.

QUOTE UNQUOTE

[The Irish are] one race of people for whom psychoanalysis is of no use whatsoever.
Sigmund Freud, psychoanalyst

THE TROUBLES

Northern Ireland consists of six (out of nine) Ulster counties in the north-east of the island. Ireland was split into two entities when the 26-county Irish Free State came into being in 1922. This happened after a war of independence, known to the Irish as 'The Troubles'.

Northern Ireland is part of the United Kingdom of Great Britain and Northern Ireland. It is subject to the same laws as Britain, and it was ruled until 1972 by a devolved Assembly located at Stormont.

Continuing agitation, both military and political, saw direct rule being imposed from Westminster through the Northern Ireland Secretary of the day.

In 1999, power was devolved to a Northern Ireland Assembly, but this was suspended in 2002. Fresh Assembly elections provided elected representatives of the people, but little progress was made in getting the participants to work together in the Assembly.

Since 2004, the British and the Irish governments have been engaged in diplomatic discussions aimed at getting the Northern Ireland Assembly up and running once more.

RELICS

St Michan's Church in Dublin contains a collection of mummified bodies stored in the vaults. The limestone in the ground keeps the air dry and helps their preservation. The remains of many of the leaders of the 1798 Rebellion are buried in the vaults.

NEVER SHORT OF A WELL-TURNED PHRASE:

Six more Gaelic sayings

May the cat eat you and the devil eat the cat
Go n-ithe an cat thú is go n-ithe an diabhal an cat

A country without a language, a country without a soul
Tír gan teanga, tír gan anam

Ireland forever
Éireann go Brách

Your house is your castle
Is é do bhaile do chaisleán

Laziness is a heavy burden
Is trom an t-ualach an leisce

A hint is sufficient for the wise
Is leor nod don eolach

RECORD BREAKERS

The oldest athlete to win an Olympic title was Irish-born Patrick Joseph 'Babe' McDonald. He was 42 years and 26 days old when he won the 56lb (25.4kg) weight throw at Antwerp, Belgium, on 21 August 1920. McDonald represented the USA on the day.

GONE BUT NOT FORGOTTEN

Anna Livia – was nicknamed Floozie in the Jacuzzi
The bronze monument was located on O'Connell Street in Dublin. A woman sat on a slope with water flowing past her as a personification of the River Liffey. It was removed in 2001 and is to be re-located.

A Flowerbed on Dublin's O'Connell Bridge was nicknamed the Tomb of the Unknown Gurrier
The very large flowerbed on Dublin's O'Connell Bridge resembled a long grave and a gurrier was a Dublin urchin. It was removed in the 1950s.

---

142 *Number of new trees planted on Dublin's O'Connell Street in 2006 to replace others removed during refurbishment*

I'm an Irish Catholic and I have a long iceberg of guilt.
Edna O'Brien, Irish novelist and short story writer

TITANIC MOVIES

A made-for-television film on the sinking of the Belfast-built Titanic was shown in 1979 starring David Janssen and Cloris Leachman. Another made-for-TV movie premiered in 1996 and starred George C Scott and Marilu Henner

Raise the Titanic was released in 1980. It was based on a novel by Clive Cussler and was a flop and almost sank the studio. Lew Grade, one of its major backers, said it would have been cheaper to lower the Atlantic than to make the film.

IRISH RIDDLE

Which Irishman invented a popular shorthand system?
Answer on page 153.

THE ORANGE ORDER

The Orange Order is the largest Protestant organisation in Northern Ireland. Its estimated membership of 60,000–80,000 belongs to regional lodges, which are based on those of the Masonic Order. As well as lodges in Ireland, the Orange Order also has lodges in Scotland and the US. Many are guarded by secret password and notoriously difficult to join.

The order was founded on 21 September 1795 after a 15-minute skirmish between Protestants and Catholics at the 'Battle of the Diamond' in Loughgall, Co Armagh. Daniel Winter, James Wilson and James Sloan formed the Orange Order after the battle to protect Protestant property.

The name of the order was chosen to remember the victory of Protestant King William of Orange over Catholic King James in the Battle of the Boyne in 1690.

As part of its mission to protect Protestant ascendancy in Northern Ireland the Orange Order holds annual parades to show its allegiance to the crown from Easter until 12 July every year. Marchers traditionally wear bowler hats and orange sashes.

DEPARTED STATUES

A statue of Queen Victoria who died in 1901 stood in the forecourt of Leinster House, the seat of the *Oireachtas Éireann* (Irish Parliament). The statue was removed to storage in 1947. It was sold to the city of Sydney in Australia in the late 1980s.

A statue of Lord Horatio Nelson stood atop a dominant 36.8m pillar beside the GPO on O'Connell Street. Erected three years after his death in 1808, it was blown up by the IRA in 1966, just weeks before the fiftieth anniversary of the Easter Rising. The Irish army blew up the stump and caused more window breakages in the process.

IRISH INVENTIONS

Co Down man James Martin invented the world's first ejector seat. His device was first tested using a crash dummy in 1945. In 1946 Bernard Lynch became the first person to participate in a live test. James Bond had a car once with an ejector seat on the passenger side.

Navan-born Francis Beaufort, conceived the wind force scale that now bears his name. A distinguished naval commander, his 13-point Scale was adopted by the British navy in 1838. He was knighted for his achievement.

Monaghan-born John Robert Gregg invented a shorthand system of speed writing in 1888. The Gregg system modelled the mechanics and positioning of traditional writing. It was later adapted to several other languages. Using the system, people can see what they said in writing, which is neat, and fast.

IRISH SOCCER

Ireland qualified for 1990 World Cup in Italy, where they progressed to the quarterfinals. After drawing all three of their opening group matches, Ireland beat Romania in a 5-4 penalty shoot. In the quarterfinals, Ireland faced hosts, Italy, in Rome, but lost 1-0.

Ireland qualified for their second World Cup finals in succession in 1994 under Jack Charlton. In New York's Giants Stadium Ireland took revenge on Italy for defeat in 1990. Ultimately Ireland were beaten 2-0 by Holland and were out. Jack Charlton resigned just after Christmas to be replaced by his captain Mick McCarthy.

RECORD BREAKERS

The youngest rugby league international player up to 2006 was
Gavin Gordon who played for Ireland vs Moldova. The match was
played on 16 October 1995 at Spotland, Rochdale, England.
Gordon was aged 17 years and 229 days on the day.

The late Joey Dunlop had a record 26 victories in the Isle of Man
TT races between 1977 and 2000. Five times World Motorcycle
Champion, Dunlop was killed in an accident while racing in 2000
in Estonia.

Paddy Doyle covered a distance of 1.6 kilometres with a rucksack
weighing 18.1 kilograms on his back, in five minutes 35 seconds at
Ballycotton, Co Cork on 7 March 1993. A multiple record holder
Paddy retired from record events in 2001.

James Devine, from Limerick, tapped out a world record of
38 taps per second in Sydney, Australia, in May 1998.
In shoes that is.

All 12 members of the Irwin family collectively ran the Dublin
marathon in 1995. Mary, Catherine, Frank, Katrina, Patricia,
Josephine, Veronica, Rosemary, Margaret, Cecilia, Barry and
Marthin all ran or walked in memory of their father, who was a
regular Dublin Marathon participant. Geraldine was the last Irwin
across the line in a time of 7:37:04.

TALKING MOVIES

The Dingle peninsula was the scene of Oscar-winning cinematography
in the 1970s film *Ryan's Daughter*. It starred Robert Mitchum, Sarah
Miles, Trevor Howard, John Mills and Christopher Jones. Mills won
an Oscar for his portrayal of a crippled mute in the movie. He said
nothing and won an Oscar for doing so.

QUOTE UNQUOTE

Love is never defeated, and I could add,
the history of Ireland proves it.
Pope John Paul II (1920-2005), Polish pontiff, in a speech to the
people of Galway in 1979

Number of young people who received Young Citizen Award pins at an 145
Uachtaráin in 2006 from President McAleese

FILMS ABOUT IRELAND

Angela's Ashes (2000)
The bestselling autobiography by Irish expat Frank McCourt brought to the screen, depicting the poverty endemic in the slums of pre-war Limerick.

Bloody Sunday (2002)
Paul Greengrass's harrowing film about the events of Sunday 30 January 1972, when 26 Irish Civil Rights protestors were shot by members of 2nd Batallion of the British Parachute Regiment during a Northern Ireland Civil Rights Association march in Derry, Northern Ireland.

Michael Collins (1996)
The story of Michael Collins who helped establish the Irish Free State in the 1920s, but was later vilified for his input.

The Commitments (1991)
Jimmy Rabbitte's attempt to form the 'World's Hardest Working Band' and bring soul music to the people of Dublin.

The Crying Game (1992)
Neil Jordan's brilliant tale of a friendship between Fergus, an Irish Republican Army volunteer, and Jody, a kidnapped British soldier.

In the Name of the Father (1994)
A moving tale of a man wrongly imprisoned for an IRA bombing in the 1970s.

A Man of No Importance (1994)
The extraordinary story of a poetic bus conductor who dreams of staging Oscar Wilde's plays in 1960s Dublin.

The Magdalene Sisters (2002)
The fictional stories of three Irish girls sent to the Magdalene sisterhood asylum to correct their 'sins'.

IRISH WORDS

The term 'lynch-law' is said to owe its origin to James Fitzstephen Lynch, the Mayor and Warden of Galway, who tried and executed his own son, Walter, in 1493. His son was found guilty of murder.

RELICS

St Oliver Plunkett's head rests in a glass shrine in St Peter's Church, in Drogheda. He was a seventeenth century Archbishop of Armagh, and was executed in 1691. Plunkett was arrested and charged with partaking in a 'Popish plot' with Richard Power, Earl of Tyrone and it was all downhill after that.

WRITERS' TAX ALLOWANCE

A no-limit tax exemption for writers and artists was introduced by the late Charlie Haughey TD, while he was Minister for Finance in 1969.

His party colleague, Brian Cowen TD, as Minister for Finance in 2006, capped artists' tax exemption at a level of €250,000 in any one tax year.

The exemption always applied only to approved works and was not a general exemption from taxation for the writer.

Half of all writers and other artists who qualified in 2001 for income tax exemption earned less than €10,000 in artistic income in that year, according to the Revenue Commissioners.

In a submission opposing the capping of the exemption, the Irish Writers' Union said the exemption facilitated start-up writers and encouraged them to persevere in their careers. It said the getting-established period requires an enormous investment of a writer's time over many years, with very little or no income being generated from writing in the early years.

Cowen capped earnings nevertheless.

SAILING AHEAD

Kildare-born Ernest Shackleton led Antarctic expeditions in the early twentieth century. He was knighted by King Edward VII for so doing. Shackleton died of a heart attack on board his ship, the *Quest*, while anchored off South Georgia on 5 January 1922.

QUOTE UNQUOTE

All the world's a stage and most of us are desperately unrehearsed.
Sean O'Casey, Irish dramatist and memoirist

Ireland rugby shirt, £8
Embroidered Shamrock to chest and embroidered Flag to reverse
(seven by five centimetres) with words 'The Craic' under flag.

***An Apology for the British Government in Ireland*, MH Gill, £9**
Published in Dublin by MH Gill & Son, 1920, 90 pages. Famine,
United Irishmen, Orangism, Orange Order, Sinn Féin etc. Very good
copy, pages browned.

Picture Map Puzzle of Ireland, 500-piece Jigsaw, £4.50
Ideal as a picture or learning tool.

Guinness Ireland Music hard enamel authentic pin badge, £0.99
This design was produced to highlight Guinness and music and was
used in the early 1990s by Guinness Ireland as a giveaway in bars
before and during the Cork Jazz Festival.

'I luv Ireland' beanie bear soft toy, £0.99
Immaculate condition. Any questions, just ask.

'Learn the Belfast Lingo' shirt, £3.50
Have a laugh at our expense – we don't mind – we do it too!

Two Russ trolls in sweatshirts, 'I love Ireland' and 'Ryanair', £1.99
Two cute Russ Trolls, both are about five inches tall. Both are
wearing sweatshirts, one with 'I love Ireland' with green sleeves and
the other is 'Ryanair Ireland' with blue sleeves.

Ireland guitar pick, £0.75
Medium thickness guitar pick bearing an Irish shamrock

George Best Northern Ireland Football Memorial Shirt, £8.99
The world's greatest football legend was always proud of his Belfast
roots – you too can be proud and honour his memory by wearing
this shirt.

TOMBS

Excavation findings from the 3,500BC passage tomb Mound of the
Hostages at Tara, Co Meath included human bones, and artefacts.
The tomb consists of three successive compartments separated by low
sill stones, the roof stones cover two inner compartments.

OLD PICTURE, NEW CAPTION

*David never quite followed the thread
of the Irishman's stories.*

IRISH WORDS

The word 'boycott' means to shun. It was a tactic used against Captain Boycott (1832-1897), a land agent in Co Mayo during agrarian unrest.

AN IRISH FIRST

Former submarine commander in the British navy, Bill King was the first Irishman to sail alone around the world. The westward voyage began in 1970 and concluded in 1973. King's vessel, the *Galway Blazer II*, was a plywood schooner measuring 12.8 by 3.13 metres.

WINNERS OF THE INTERNATIONAL IMPAC DUBLIN LITERARY AWARD

2006 *The Master* by Colm Tóibín

2005 *The Known World* by Edward P Jones

2004 *This Blinding Absence of Light* by Tahar Ben Jelloun
(translated from the French by Linda Coverdale)

2003 *My Name is Red* by Orhan Pamuk
(translated from the Turkish by Orhan Pamuk)

2002 *Atomised (or The Elementary Particles)*
by Michel Houellebecq
(translated from the French by Frank Wynne)

2001 *No Great Mischief* by Alastair MacLeod

2000 *Wide Open* by Nicola Barker

1999 *Ingenious Pain* by Andrew Miller

1998 *The Land of Green Plums* by Herta Müller
(translated from the German by Michael Hofmann)

1997 *A Heart So White* by Javier Marías
(translated from the Spanish by Margaret Jull Costa)

1996 *Remembering Babylon* by David Malouf

IRISH UNDERSTATEMENT

'He was his own worst enemy': is usually directed at a recently dead bowsie that nobody liked and whom most are just as glad to see moving on to the next life.

A LIBRARY FOR THE NATION

The first public library in Ireland was named for Narcissus Marsh who founded the library in 1701. It was still in operation in 2006.

150 *Amount in tonnes of arms intercepted by French navy aboard the Eksund sailing from Libya to the IRA in 1987*

DURING THE COMPILATION OF THIS BOOK, THE COMPANION TEAM...

Lived off a diet of Guinness and potatoes and are now auditioning for the next series of *Fat Nation*

Visited Giant's Causeway, but were disappointed to find no giants

Counted the number of times their Irish acquaintances used the word 'grand'. The average was three times a sentence

Tried to learn an Irish jig, much to the amusement of the locals

Went for a swim in the Irish Sea, but only managed to last for 30 seconds before they lost feeling in their fingers and toes

Asked an Irishman for directions and ended up where they'd started

Bet on the horses expecting that the luck of the Irish might rub off on them; unfortunately the horse they backed fell at the first fence

Visited Dublin for St Patrick's Day, but don't remember much about it

Developed a taste for Irish coffee, which helped livened up the office

Please note that although every effort has been made to ensure accuracy in this book, the above statistics may be the results of whiskey-soaked minds

I have never met anyone in Ireland who understood the Irish Question, except one Englishman who had only been there a week.
Keith Fraser, English MP

The answers. As if you needed them.

P 20. Arthur Wellesley, Duke of Wellington was born in Dublin in 1769

P 32. James Joyce opened The Volta, in Dublin, on 20 December 1909.

P 39. Count Dracula, created by Dubliner Bram Stoker (1847–1912). The Count or his immediate descendants outnumber those of his closest rival, Frankenstein's creation, by 162 to 117.

P 45. St Patrick.

P 53. Setanta which was the original name of Cúchulainn, a mythical Irish warrior who single-handedly defended the province of Ulster when his companions were struck down under a magic spell.

P 59. Rody Doyle in 1993 with *Paddy Clarke Ha Ha Ha*.

P 72. There is no such thing as a mandatory 'life sentence'. It is a matter for the courts to decide for how long someone should be detained.

P 78. Sean McBride (1904-1988) He fought in the Irish War of Independence from 1919 to 1921. He received the 1974 Nobel Prize for his work as chairman of both Amnesty International and the International Peace Bureau in Geneva; the American Medal of Justice (1975) for his humanitarian work for peace and the Lenin Peace Prize (1977) for co-creating Amnesty International.

P 89. j k q v w x y z.

P 95. In Temple Bar Dublin.

P 102. Eamon de Valera.

P 106. William Joyce, Lord Haw Haw, who broadcast propaganda in English for Nazi Germany

P 118. Hibernia

P 128. Chaim Herzog, sixth President of Israel, was born in Belfast in 1918

P 130. Ireland's first railway from Dublin to Kingstown built in 1834 was the world's first commuter line.

Number of priests who fled Wicklow in 1698 through Dublin ahead of 153
coercive penal laws outlawing their religion

P 140. The French Baron de Forest established a world record of 85.9 miles per hour during speed trials in Dublin's Phoenix Park in 1903.

P 143. John Robert Gregg from County Monaghan invented the internationally used Gregg Shorthand System.

BIBLIOGRAPHY

Birds of Ireland *www.birdwatchireland.ie*

Central Statistics Office *www.cso.ie*

Citizens' information online *www.oasis.gov.ie*

Central Fisheries Board *www.cfb.ie*

Gaelic Athletic Association *www.gaa.ie*

Guinness world records *www.guinnessworldrecords.com*

History magazine and website *www.historyireland.com*

Irish Sea Fisheries Board *www.bim.ie*

Killarney National Park *www.npws.ie*

National police force history *www.esatclear.ie/~garda*

Nobel Prize *http://nobelprize.org*

Office of Public Works *www.opw.ie*

Phoenix Park history and guidebook *www.liffey-i.com*

Presidents past and present and official residence *www.president.ie*

Soccer body for Republic *www.fai.ie*

Soccer body for Northern Ireland *www.irishfa.com*

ACKNOWLEDGEMENTS

We gratefully acknowledge permission to reprint extracts of copyright material in this book from the following authors, publishers and executors:

Extract from The Diary of Virginia Woolf, Volume IV *(1931-1935) by Virginia Woolf, published by Hogarth Press. World Rights, excluding US, by kind permission of the executors of the Virginia Woolf Estate and the Random House Group Limited. US permission © 1982 by kind permission of Quentin Bell and Angelica Garnett, reprinted by permission of Harcourt, Inc.*

Windharp *by John Monatague, published by The Gallery Press, by kind permission of the author and The Gallery Press.*

Extract from The Matter with Ireland *by George Bernard Shaw, by kind permission of the University Press of Florida.*

Extract from Ireland, A Bicycle, and A Tin Whistle *by David A Wilson, by kind permission of McGill-Queen's University Press.*

Extract from Collected Stories *by Elizabeth Bowen reproduced with kind permission of Curtis Brown Group Ltd, London, on behalf of the Estate of Elizabeth Bowen.*

Extract from In Search of Ireland *by HV Morton, by kind permission of Methuen Publishing Ltd.*

The Lake Isle of Innisfree, *WB Yeats, reprinted by permission of AP Watt Ltd on behalf of Michael B Yeats for UK and World Rights. By courtesy of Dover publications for US Rights.*

INDEX

FILL YOUR BOOKSHELF AND YOUR MIND

The Birdwatcher's Companion Twitchers, birders and ornithologists are all catered for in this unique book. ISBN 1-86105-833-0

The Cook's Companion Foie gras or fry-ups, this tasty compilation is an essential ingredient in any kitchen. ISBN 1-86105-772-5

The Countryside Companion From milking stools to crofters tools, this book opens the lid on the rural scene. ISBN 1-86105-918-3

The Fishing Companion This fascinating catch of fishy facts offers a whole new angle on angling. ISBN 1-86105-919-1

The Gardener's Companion For anyone who has ever gone in search of flowers, beauty and inspiration. ISBN 1-86105-771-7

The Golfer's Companion From plus fours to six irons, here's where to find the heaven and hell of golf. ISBN 1-86105-834-9

The History of Britain Companion All the oddities, quirks, origins and stories that make our country what it is today. ISBN 1-86105-914-0

The Ideas Companion The stories behind the trademarks, inventions, and brands that we come across every day. ISBN 1-86105-835-7

The Legal Companion From lawmakers to lawbreakers, find out all the quirks and stories behind the legal world. ISBN 1-86105-838-1

The Literary Companion Literary fact and fiction from Rebecca East to Vita Sackville-West. ISBN 1-86105-798-9

The London Companion Explore the history and mystery of the most exciting capital city in the world. ISBN 1-86105-799-7

The Moviegoer's Companion Movies, actors, cinemas and salty popcorn in all their glamorous glory. ISBN 1-86105-797-0

The Politics Companion Great leaders and greater liars of international politics gather round the hustings. ISBN 1-86105-796-2

The Sailing Companion Starboards, stinkpots, raggie and sterns – here's where to find out more. ISBN 1-86105-839-X

The Shakespeare Companion A long, hard look at the man behind the moustache and his plethora of works. ISBN 1-86105-913-2

The Traveller's Companion For anyone who's ever stared at a plane and spent the day dreaming of faraway lands. ISBN 1-86105-773-3

The Walker's Companion Ever laced a sturdy boot and stepped out in search of stimulation? This book is for you. ISBN 1-86105-825-X

The Wildlife Companion Animal amazements and botanical beauties abound in this book of natural need-to-knows. ISBN 1-86105-770-9